CARL   ORFF

The Schulwerk

THE SCHULWERK is Volume 3 of Carl Orff/DOCUMENTATION, His Life and Works, an eight volume autobiography of Carl Orff.

© 1976 Hans Schneider, D8132 Tutzing, W. Germany

English Edition © 1978 Schott Music Corp., New York

(Translated by Margaret Murray)

ISBN 0-930448-06-5

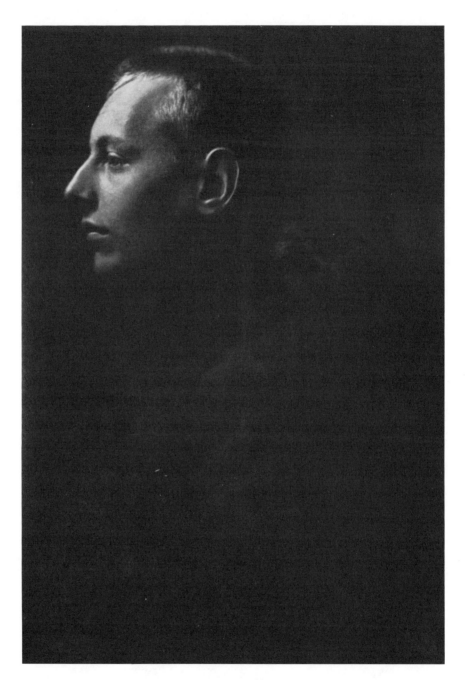

Carl Orff · 1923

Contents

Appendix

THE NEW DANCE MOVEMENT

"Dance stands nearest to the roots of all the arts."

In the first decades of this century it seemed to me as if a spring storm were sweeping through the city of Munich. It rushed down the Ludwigsstrasse through the Siegestor, roared down the Leopoldstrasse and in Schwabing (a district of Munich) it took with it, helter-skelter, enthusiastic young poets, writers, painters and musicians. It was Schwabing that became a stronghold for young, forward-looking artists and, not least, provided a home for the "New Dance Movement" that caused a great stir. Rudolf von Delius wrote about this time in 1925:

"It was March 1914 in Munich. The new dance movement had been set in motion with the names: Duncan, Wiesenthal, St. Dénis, Derp, Sacharoff. Inhibitions were overcome and everyone wanted to dance; every girl with a good figure practised physical culture eagerly, hired a hall and presented herself. Yet again someone had sent me free tickets. I was tired of and disappointed by all this amateurism and yet I wanted to go just once more. I sent the other ticket to a friend who was an art historian; In the first interval I suggested that we leave. My companion hesitated. 'There is a lady here who is also a dancer. I would at least like to introduce you to her.' I was suddenly aware of two eyes beside me: suffering, disdain, pride. My friend said: 'Mary Wigman.' As we said good-bye she invited me: she wanted to show me something in her studio: experiments and sketches. I arrived at her address in the Schwanenthalerstrasse: an almost empty room; in the corner a screen for changing; drums, rattles, recorders. 'My music', she said. Suddenly she stood there. Wild, tall, electric. Almost like fury. And she danced the witches' dance. She danced other things too: dreamlike tenderness. Now I knew everything. She was the greatest dancer of the time."

At that time Mary Wigman had finished her period of study with Dalcroze in Hellerau, a study that had not satisfied her. Dalcroze was not a dancer. Mary Wigman sought dance in its absolute state. Not a kind of dance that, like ivy, needed music as a house to climb on and took it for granted. She found it with Rudolf von Laban whom she sought out in his circle of pupils in Ascona.

For both Wigman and Laban the meeting in Ascona was a fateful encounter. In 1914 Wigman became Laban's secretary and assistant in Zürich. There followed many years of intensive work and Laban and Wigman became the initiators and perfectors of "Modern Dance".

It took several years before Wigman was able to put across her highly personal and novel art form. The first "musicless" dances were produced, "musicless" as they were then described. For me, though, an ostinato on a throbbing timpani or a ringing gong did constitute music.

After various solo evenings in Switzerland Wigman undertook a first tour of Germany with varying response but with growing understanding from the public. In 1920 in Dresden she founded her own school, the Wigman-Schule, and formed a dance group. She made her first tour of the United States in 1930 with the immediate, unparalleled success that continued in all her undertakings.

What Wigman had first called "Ausdruckstanz" (Expressive Dance) and "Deutscher Tanz" (German Dance) now became known throughout the world as "New German Dance". Her large group compositions lay nearest to her heart and these she took from triumph to triumph.

In her records she writes: "Out of our feeling for the times the emphasis must lie on the group dance. It is not the solo accomplishment that is the future begetter. Even with the most gifted dancer that will always be a one time, purely personal peak of achievement. The young generation of dancers should identify themselves with the group dance, as that is where the future opportunities lie. In the heart of every genuine dancer lives the idea of a theatre of the future which would include dance as one of its basic elements in a great, dramatic, combined happening. And so we dancers of today dream of a theatre that not only endorses the reason for our existence, but that allows us to work and build together a form of expression that later generations may perhaps once more perceive and experience as 'cultic' ".

The art of Mary Wigman was very significant for me and my later work. All her dances were animated by an unprecedented musicality, even the "musicless" witches' dance. She could make music with her body and transform music into corporeality. I felt that her dancing was elemental. I, too, was searching for the elemental, for elemental music.

Her group dances were still partly based on a conventional piano accompaniment and she would always add more and more exotic percussion instruments and flutes, that, coming from Far Eastern or African cultures, were all related to the dance and matched it perfectly.

Will Götze, an outstanding musician and extremely gifted with a sympathetic understanding for dance, composed the greater part of the musical accompaniments which cannot be separated from Wigman's work.

All this gave me new insights and a new outlook even if my own work belonged elsewhere. As a musician I obeyed different laws.

Today Mary Wigman's talented work is already history.

PLANS ABOUT PLANS

In 1923 Dorothee Günther came to Munich. Mutual friends in Hamburg had arranged a meeting for us during the first days of her visit. In Günther I found an alert, clear mind, full of new ideas, plans and expectations. I had an immediate rapport with her.

She described her earlier work as painter and illustrator, her attempts at becoming a writer and her time training as a producer at the state theatre in Hamburg. She also talked about her drawing studies in the life class at the art school that had given her so many disappointing impressions of stunted movement capability, so that from then on the idea of creating an organic movement education would not leave her in peace. She had turned to the then new form of physical education, Mensendieck Gymnastics, and also came to know the work of Dalcroze and Laban. She told of her journeys giving courses and lectures at the Mensendieck training centres in Berlin, Breslau, Hamburg and elsewhere, and of her invitation to give such courses in Munich, a city for which she hinted that she had great plans in mind.

I invited her to a further talk and in the form of a guest's gift she brought me a copy of a newly published volume of old music, the compositions of the recently discovered Vincent Lübeck, who had been such a well-known organist in his day. And so we came to talking about old music. I played her part of my arrangement of Monteverdi's Orfeo and I was very taken by her reaction which showed an unusual understanding. It was just then that I was looking for someone to help me with the making of a new and free German text. Several attempts with experienced librettists had come to nothing. In response to my request for help Günther thought that such a task would interest her. I had no idea then of what was to develop out of such a collaboration.

Our work on the Orfeo text advanced rapidly. The beginning was not easy for there were so many possibilities. As always with me countless versions were made until I felt that I had found the right one.

10

Dorothee Günther, 1923

From time to time Günther kept coming back to her Munich plans that became more and more concrete. Through her lectures, articles and courses she was known as an authority on the subject of movement. The various modern training centres and schools represented and laid emphasis one-sidedly only on *their* method. Günther imagined a school where various kinds of modern physical education and dance training could be offered. A specially designed course for every kind of talent. She was considering three branches of study — gymnastics, rhythmic dance and expressive dance — preceded by a basic training taken by everyone.

Oskar Lang, my senior by ten years, belonged to my circle of friends. He was an art historian and wrote about music, an idealist, an enthusiast and a free-living man, a rare combination of a genuine Schwabing Bohemian and a type like the poet Matthias Claudius. He was equally at home in theatre, concert hall or in the Pinakothek, Munich's most important picture gallery. He wrote a widely noticed book about Bruckner and wrote the preparatory introductions that I gave to the performances of my arrangements of Monteverdi. As a genuine inhabitant of Schwabing he was interested in all new things and was to be seen at most dance evenings. I therefore took the opportunity of introducing him to Günther. They understood one another immediately.

In the mean time Günther's ideas about founding a school were maturing further and Lang was just the person to give advice. He knew Bode and his school just as he was familar with the Dalcroze training. The music that they both discussed was not the kind of music that we had imagined; they were more tied to the style of one particular period of the past. So Günther was lacking music teachers for the rhythmic dance training.

One evening in Lang's presence the conversation came round once more to her school and I described how I thought the music teaching should go hand in hand with the movement teaching. I spoke about elemental music and its significance for movement education and I drew up a plan for an "Elemental Music Practice" that would only be suitable in a movement school.

As a musician I was interested in trying out a new way of teaching music. I felt that the school they were planning would give me the ideal means for such an experiment. Without considering in any way what had previously been accomplished in this field I wanted to tackle the problem in *my* way. This meant that the starting point was an artistic rather than a purely educational one.

Günther was very impressed by my outlined sketch and promised me that if her plans were realised she would work out the curriculum for music education according to my suggestions and co-ordinate them with the rest. Lang also thought that a practicable approach had been found. I later committed my ideas, more thought out in detail, to paper. Everything else could only be clarified through practical application. The whole undertaking would be breaking new ground with the future in view and would be determined, as I hoped, by time.

Many discussions followed with frequent precipitate ideas and considerations. There was always an unusual atmosphere — I can only compare it with that pre-Spring feeling, everything full of tension and expectation, waiting for the new start, all discussion, thoughts and ideas.

FOUNDING THE GÜNTHERSCHULE

It was to become a reality. In August 1923 the Mensendieck Society in Diessen am Ammersee organised a holiday course with practical work, lectures and discussions. Günther gave an excellent lecture about her ideas for a new training school and then asked me to outline my thoughts about a corresponding music training. My impromptu talk found the same considerable response as Günther's lecture. I spoke mercilessly of the deficient or out of date musical activity that was customary in most gymnastic schools, and I gave an imaginary picture of how I would change and renew it all. After a lively discussion in which I was easily able to convince the remaining sceptics, Günther was given a free hand. It was decided to open a school in Munich that Günther would direct according to the plans that we had presented.

In the same autumn I went to Berlin to Curt Sachs, who had long been internationally famous as the director of the Staatlichen Musikinstrumenten-Sammlung (State Collection of Musical Instruments). I wanted to show him my Monteverdi arrangements that had resulted from his stimulus. He described them as bold, new versions, gave me some advice, in particular that I should carry on working in this way. In the course of conversation I told him of my intention of working in a gymnastic and dance school that had just been founded. At first Sachs found the idea unusual, if not misguided, but as I further described what I had in mind he even found it interesting. "With your plan you are following aims that are entirely your own and you intend by these means to reach sources that are otherwise neglected or overlooked. You want to find the source of all beginnings. The more I think of it the more I believe that you of all people will by this means receive important stimuli for the music and your ideas. The elemental is your element, and, if I understand your far-reaching exposition correctly, you will rediscover it there."

He then invited me to a walk through his collection. It made me feel giddy to realise all that he could tell of the countless instruments from all over the world and from every epoch of "Music and Dance". His incidental remark that he was working on a world history of dance made me listen attentively and it explained his positive attitude to my plans. The knowledge that I had found Sachs as helper, friend and adviser for my new balancing act was reassuring.

On the way home my head was buzzing with ideas. "In the beginning was the drum", Sachs had said as we parted . . .

The current inflation period was not exactly favourable for such an undertaking as the founding of a school. Nevertheless we were lucky, and Günther's skill enabled us to procure the necessary teachers and rooms, our greatest problem.

After a long search we found premises at No. 21 Luisenstrasse, a one-storied, long building at the back of a courtyard. On its upper floor there was a roomy hall, with smaller neighbouring rooms for cloakroom, office and staffroom and one larger room for theory studies. We opened the school in September 1924, starting with seventeen female students between the ages of 18 and 22. The training was designed to last from two to three years. Apart from this there were evening courses for over one hundred non-professional students.

There was no money for advertising but Günther's name attracted like a magnet. The number of students grew noticeably at the beginning of each semester. Our rooms were soon inadequate and we had to double our space by making use of the lower floor of our building. Besides Günther, who directed the school and taught all theoretical subjects, and myself, who was responsible for all the music, there were three other teachers for gymnastics, rhythmics and dance. We were all filled with an optimism that corresponded to our age. Our start was a fortunate one.

Nubian female dancers

16

ELEMENTAL MUSIC

"In the beginning was the drum."

The drum induces dance. Dance has the closest relationship to music. My idea and the task that I had set myself was a regeneration of music through movement, through dance.

It is difficult to teach rhythm. One can only release it. Rhythm is no abstract concept, it is life itself. Rhythm is active and produces effects, it is the unifying power of language, music and movement.

We began with hand-clapping, finger-snapping and stamping in forms and combinations that ranged from simple to difficult and that could be integrated in many different ways into the movement lessons.

We also used rattles. "Rattles belong to the most ancient instruments of mankind." (Curt Sachs)

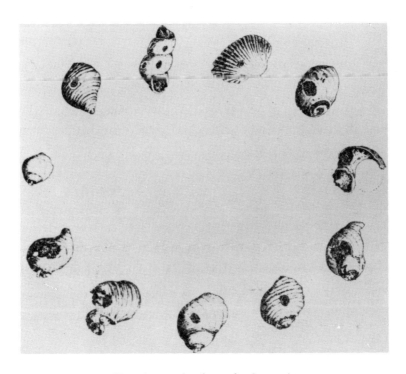

Hanging rattles from the Stone Age

We made ourselves strung rattles that could be worn on wrist, knee or ankle (on one or both sides of the body) and we used exotic models, mostly African, that could be found in every folklore museum. We used small stones, shells, snail shells, dried fruits, nut shells, and wooden balls in all possible sizes.

Strung rattles using seeds

We sewed together small and large jingles that could easily be found in the west. These primitive sound sources could have an exciting effect when used with rhythmic movement exercises and with dancing.

Single-skinned frame drums or tambours in various sizes, thought of in the first instance as accompanying instruments for dance, were struck with the hand and therefore called 'hand drums'. The many different possible qualities of sound that could be achieved by playing with a flat hand, with individual fingers, with the ball of the thumb, in the centre of the skin, at the edge of the skin, stopped or free-sounding, made for a technique of playing full of nuances that could be further extended by the use of drum-sticks as well as the hand.

Apart from the simple tambour and tambourine we used double-skinned drums that were held on the knee while sitting, or placed on a stand. They were played sideways with both hands or struck from above.

Ostinato begleitrhythmen tum Tanz mit Fussrasseln over Fussschellen.
! = rechter Fuss, q = linker Fuss

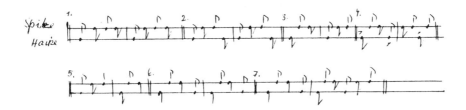

Tanz begleitung als Kombination von Singen, Klatschen u. Fussrhythmen

Drum practice

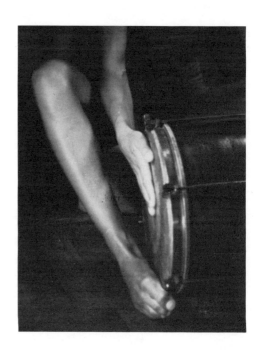

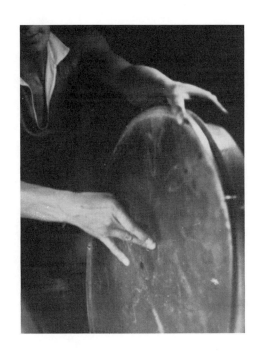

Playing double-skinned drums

Improvisation is the starting point for elemental music-making. From the beginning we practised freely-made rhythmic improvisations for which simple ostinati served as foundation and stimulus.

With advanced groups I tried to build up improvisations in several parts: over an ostinato of several bars length given by rattles worn on the ankles someone would start to clap, then another, and then more and more, coming in one after the other, each with their own rhythm, sometimes leading, returning again to the background, complementary to one another or resting at appropriate times. "Wide-meshed" rhythms that bridged and held large spans together were important. Repeated practice and getting "played in" to one another was necessary for this kind of music-making. One beat gave way to another, from one rhythmic shape another was formed, like pictures in a kaleidoscope that form and then dissolve. This continuous flow of forming and dissolving was the attraction of this ensemble exercise. It was later transferred onto percussion and other instruments. Carried by the breath, whatever the limitation, a means for lively music-making was created.

22

To help with the early stages of non-metric or free improvisation I let them think of words, series of words, and sentences, and to transfer every nuance of performance, accent and tone quality onto drums. Whole "drum monologues" from thought-out texts followed as developments of this exercise. "Dialogues" were also improvised, "argumentative discussions" with several participants produced an exciting kind of game. Another result arose when one person accompanied herself on a drum while giving a predetermined or free speech, or while singing a melody, an exercise that remained reserved for the specially gifted and that demanded an accompaniment especially rich in nuances of tone and colour.

Three pieces for a speaker
who accompanies herself on a drum:

Vor meinem Fenster singt ein Vogel
(A bird sings outside my window)

Arno Holz (aus:Phantasus)

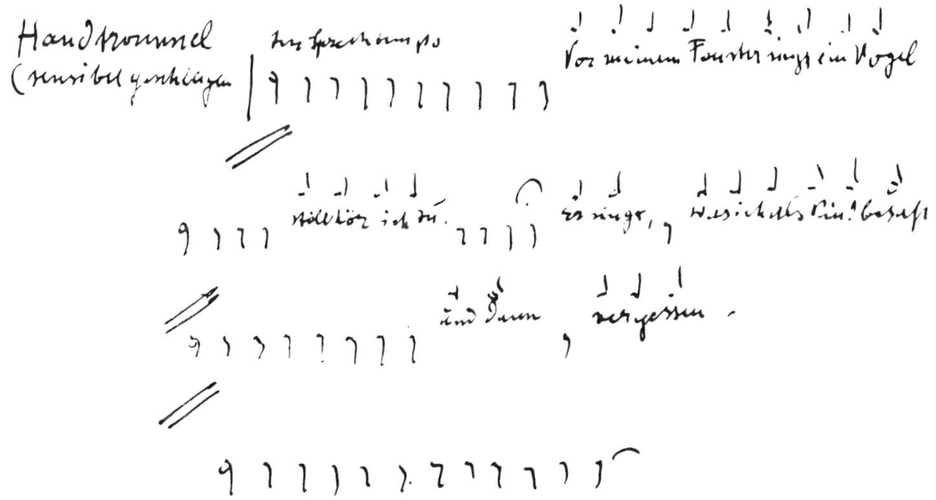

Bitte an den Schlaf, nach schwersten Studen
(An entreaty to Sleep, after the heaviest hours)

Detlev von Liliencron

Doch eh der Peitschenknall des neuen Tages
Mich morgen wieder in die Wüste ruft,
Bestelle deinen Bruder an mein Bett.

Drum ♩. ♩. ♩. ♩.

Gutmütig legt der alte Herr die Hand
Auf meine Augen, die sich öffnen wollen,
Und sagt ein Wiegenlied, die Worte langsam,
Sehr langsam sprechend:
            Nicht bange sein . . .

Still e'er the whiplash of a new day
Calls me at daybreak once more into the desert,
Ask your brother to come to my bed.

Beningly the old man lays his hand
Upon my eyes that wish to open,
And recites a lullaby, the words slowly,
Very slowly spoken:
            Have no fear . . .

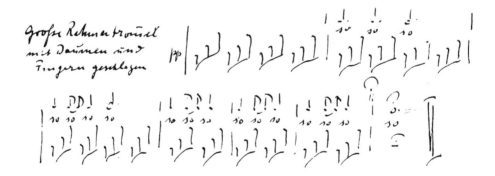

Liliencron lays out the last verse thus:
Nicht bange sein . . .
So, so . . . so . . .
So, so, so . . .

24

Zum Einschlafen zu sagen
(Rainer Maria Rilke)

Trommel

Mit etwas singender Sprechstimme.

Ich möchte jemanden einsingen, bei jemandem sitzen u. sein.

Ich möchte dich wiegen u. klein singen u. begleiten schlafaus u. schlafein.

Ich möchte der einzige sein im Haus, der wüßte: die Nacht war kalt.

Und möchte horchen herein u. hinaus, in dich, in die Welt, in den Wald.—

Die Uhren rufen sich schlagend an, man sieht der Zeit auf den Grund.

Und unten geht noch ein fremder Mann u. stört einen fremden Hund.

Dahinter wird stille. Ich habe groß die Augen auf dich gelegt;

sie halten dich sanft u. lassen dich los, wenn ein Ding sich im Dunkel bewegt.

Zum Einschlafen zu sagen
(To speak someone to sleep)

Rainer Maria Rilke

Ich möchte jemanden einsingen,
bei jemandem sitzen und sein.
Ich möchte dich wiegen und kleinsingen
und begleiten schlafaus und schlafein.
Ich möchte der einzige sein im Haus,
der wüsste: Die Nacht war kalt.
Und möchte horchen herein und hinaus
in dich, in die Welt, in den Wald. —

Die Uhren rufen sich schlagend an,
man sieht der Zeit auf den Grund.
Und unten geht noch ein fremder Mann
und stört einen fremden Hund.
Dahinter wird Stille. Ich habe gross
die Augen auf dich gelegt;
sie halten dich sanft und lassen dich los,
wenn ein Ding sich im Dunkel bewegt.

I would sing to someone,
To sit and be by their side.
I would rock you and sing
To accompany your sleeping and waking.
I would be alone in the house
To know that the night was cold.
And would listen within and without,
To you, to the world, to the forest

The clocks call each other as they chime,
And thus one is aware of time.
Down below a stranger is still walking
And he disturbs a strange dog.
After that all is quiet. With a wide glance
My eyes have rested on you;
They encompass you gently and leave you
When anything moves in the darkness.

The "incantation" needed, the singing-and-talking-someone-to-sleep is only to be achieved by those who are gifted with particular powers of suggestion. It cannot really be written down.

A large tambour or a double-headed drum is the most suitable instrument.

It is particularly in the dramatic poem or ballad that a drum can come nearest to "speech", often with a driving ostinato or with a range of sound from the most furious banging to the most delicate, individual "drops" of water. One must awaken the rhythm in the most varied ways and must "loosen the tongue" of the drum. We often tried to interpret the old Scottish ballad "Edward" or the Danish "Herr Olof" in the version by Johann Gottfried Herder.

The abundance of possibilities available in this truly elemental way of making music can neither be explained in detail nor described. I often thought with sadness of the many wonderful drums in Curt Sachs' Berlin collection, where they stood in rows, unused and condemned to be mute; so much unheard music slumbered in them.

Only in more recent days are we on the way to investigating the countless possibilities of tone colour on a drum, and are thus coming to a rediscovery of this instrument.

PIANO EXERCISES

The piano has a key position in western music, and will keep this position as long as there is such a music.

The subject "Piano exercises" was compulsory for all students in the Rhythmic and Dance departments, whether musically trained or not.

The drone is the most important and most widely found form of part singing and playing. While one voice provides the melody the other sustains one note, the key note or fundamental note, either above or below the melody. This is the prototype of our pedal note.

This drone develops itself in two directions: firstly by sustaining a chord consisting of fundamental, fifth and octave, like bagpipes or hurdy-gurdy; secondly in that the drone moves between a limited number of notes like an ostinato, the so-called "wandering drone" (after Curt Sachs)

We began with tone and touch exercises; with drone fifths in low and high registers, played loud and soft, given a rhythmic pattern, smooth or staccato, doubled, broken like an arpeggio and repeated. To these fundamental sounds that were soon filled out into larger ostinati I improvised melodies on a second piano that served as models for the students' improvisations that followed.

The next step was to have two students at one instrument, one playing the melody, the other the drone, the leading role being taken alternately by melody and drone. Finally *one* player could take over both roles simultaneously.

It was an initial style, understood by everyone and easy to copy. If the advanced student was able continually to find new possibilities, so the beginner could always be learning while she played her simple drone. Teaching this way in groups proved its value since every student could be given a task according to her ability. It depended on finding, inventing and discovering. The players had to "grow ears on the ends of their fingers"; how to give a meaningful shape to a melody and how to bring it to an end. The playing hand must acquire the "ability to shape melodies". In order to educate each hand equally, drones and melodies were played four-handed in different registers, at the octave, supplemented or extended.

28

All these exercises were continually transposed into all modes. Through the inclusion of the black notes new turns of melody became possible according to the hand structure.

Beside the ever recurring "stationary turns of speech" there developed an inexhaustible source for the making of new melodies. As playing technique improved it became possible to play paraphonically (playing the melody in parallel perfect fourths or fifths) and playing melodies in parallel thirds and sixths.

Oskar Lang, always interested in the progress of the school, visited our improvisation sessions now and then and was amazed at the rapid progress we achieved with our drone playing. On one occasion, as we had reached the stage of playing four-handed, he wanted to join us in our way of improvising. I took charge of a broadly built, resonant drone and Lang improvised at the second piano. Since he had a good technique he achieved a virtuoso effect which impressed the students considerably. Had I been alone I could not have shown him such an example.

Lang had largely made use of a way of playing that was very popular in our improvisations, *descanting:* to songs or dances that corresponded to our style we improvised, in high or middle register, free melodies that were by no means equivalent in importance to the main melody, but that rather represented extra voices that enriched the texture.

A particular kind of improvisation resulted from the use of the pentatonic scale. Over an ostinato bass several melodies could be improvised simultaneously or in question and answer phrases. We were thus able to risk improvisations on two grand pianos, with often up to four people playing, at our public student performances. Since there were no semitones in this exercise, and therefore no dissonance tensions, the different voices came together in a kind of oscillation. Once the structure of the pentatonic scale had been grasped, the improvisations arose of their own accord, with question and answer phrasing and imitation emphasising formal relationships.

We also continually improvised small forms, at first the episodes to given rondo themes, later more extended rondos. Further improvisation material arose out of the use of various dance rhythms such as Bolero, Habañera, Siciliana and others, whose marked accompanying rhythm prescribed melody and form. The Berceuse was particularly easy to manage and therefore popular.

The drone style that we developed in our piano exercises was of fundamental importance to the whole of our "elemental music exercises". It stands as antithesis to the harmonic style that rests on a functional foundation.

Individual lessons were given as well as the group lessons. They fulfilled various functions: on the one hand to give those students with no previous piano experience some technique, while on the other hand it was especially important to give the advanced students further help in order to raise the aims of the improvisation sessions.

These individual lessons could not have been called piano lessons of the usual kind but were rather music lessons that covered the whole "ballast" of music theory that could not have been handled in the group, such as keyboard harmony, cadential and figured bass, knowledge of which was essential for the improvisation of simple Malagueñas and Passacaglias.

In the long run these individual lessons proved too great a burden for me. Among my private pupils I found a most suitable candidate, the harpsichordist Anna Barbara Speckner and she was able to take these lessons over and conduct them in exactly the way I wanted. She became an important helper and colleague when the music studies were extended. Two books: "Alte englische Kontratänze" (Old English Country Dances) and "Aus alten Spielbüchern" (Taken from old collections of traditional songs) each written for keyboard instruments, are among the fruits of her educational and artistic activity.

All improvisation actually avoids written notation. The written sketch and its subsequent working out are the beginning stages of composition, and this was not our intention. The examples of notation that follow should stimulate, inform and demonstrate various possibilities in the field of elemental improvisation. They have their origin in those attempts of ours in the Güntherschule. Coming from improvisation, they should lead back again to improvisation.

Drone exercise for one and more players

I

1. A melody with the range of a fifth is underpinned by an accompaniment of simple and moving drone.

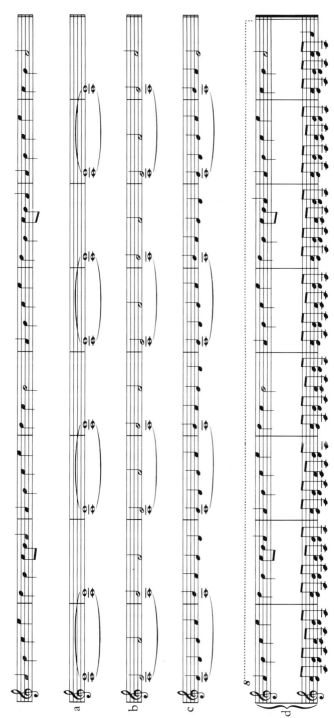

A descant part over a paraphonic melody. The drone support is accentuated through an appoggiatura. (For three players)

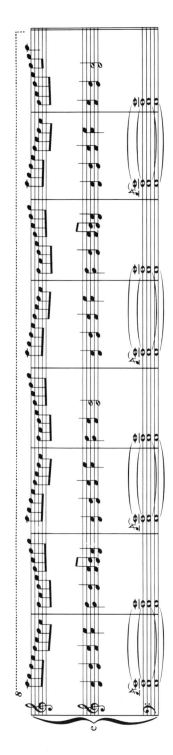

Over a different tonal foundation the melody, now doubly paraphonic, has the descant below it in a middle register.

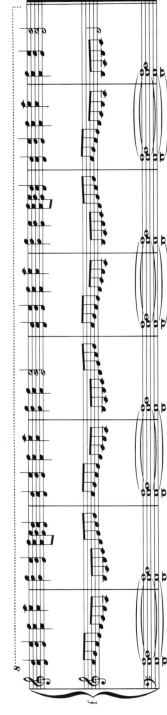

2. A melody, again with the range of a fifth, is supported by a wandering (moving) and by a broken drone.

Paraphonic melody over a sustained pedal note drone with a middle part in parallel fifths like a malagueña

d

The same melody and bass but with a descanting middle part.

e

34

3. A florid upper part in major, supported by a moving drone.

The same melody with a parallel sixth above it, and a moving drone with appoggiatura establishing a minor key

With major/minor drone

37

4. Berceuse. Over a swinging drone a melody develops:

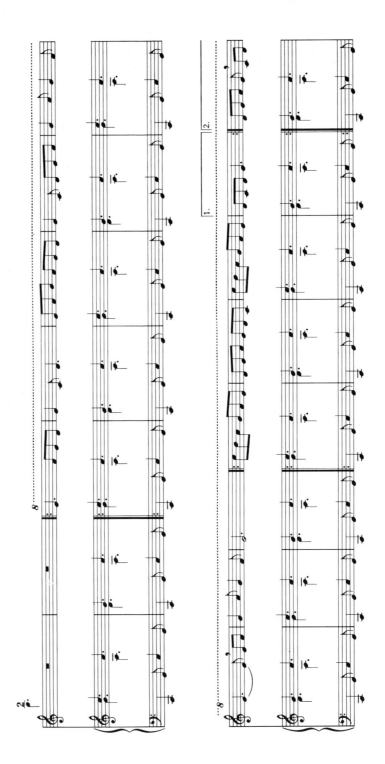

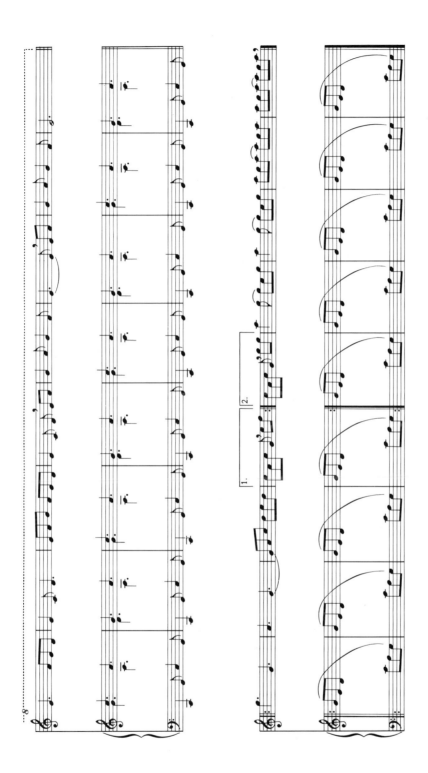

5. Berceuse (for two players on two pianos)

40

6. Ostinato exercise "All kinds of diversions".
Andante (each part can also be played at double the speed)

Melody at the same speed, ostinato twice as fast.

41

The free melody is twice as fast as the previous one.

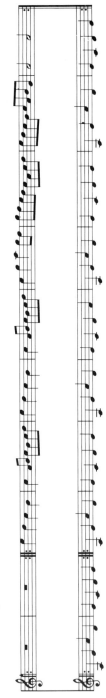

Lower part is twice as fast.

42

7. Different types of melody over a constant broken drone accompaniment (also to be worked out as a rondo)

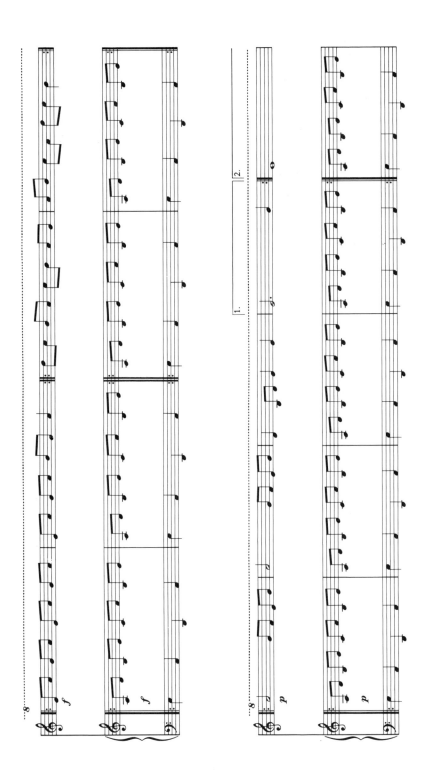

44

8. Drone in both high and low register (2 players).

46

9. (To be worked out as a rondo)

Molto allegro e forte

47

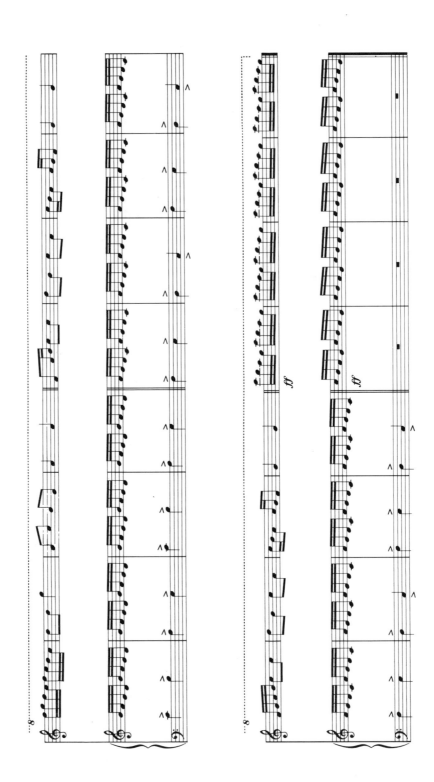

48

The foregoing examples and models illustrate a series of exercises that were used over a long period of time. The point of emphasis was always being varied and progress had to be made a step at a time.

In the first training classes a drone style was only developed on the piano; in later years the same technique was begun simultaneously on the barred instruments that had meanwhile been developed for our use, and on recorders as well. But the piano exercises were never allowed to fade quite into the background, for only on this instrument was such volume and resonance accessible.

Whereas the first group of examples is intended for beginners, the second already requires more advanced players, for since the whole range of the instrument is included, new and further possibilities for improvisation present themselves. In addition the following written examples can be used later as basic material for work with various other instruments:

No. 13 gives the first player the opportunity to extend the melody freely, while the second can spin out the episodes over the paraphonic foundation as long as he chooses.

No. 14 has pesante opening pentatonic clusters that provide a sonority into which the most abundant variety of soloistic improvisations can be built, while the continuous progress of the three-part ostinato provides a supporting foundation for linear improvisation in one or more parts. There are no time limits given either for ostinato or for improvisation. Here also, a transfer to barred instruments, recorders and other instruments would suggest itself. As a first exercise the three-part ostinato could be practised (without any overlying improvisation) so that it started in pianissimo, gradually increasing in volume for as long as desired, swelling to fortissimo, and, tracing the same path in reverse, dying away in pianissimo at the end.

No. 15 is a special task for experienced pianists who can freely enjoy to the full what is really a single line of melody (right hand doubled at the sixth and the octave, left hand in thirds with a mirror relationship to the right hand and always the same distance from it) and who can give way to every impulse.

10. Bolero

Freely develop the melody further in the same way over the same accompaniment to the end.

11. *Der Meye* (The month of May)
With simple and paraphonic descant part.

12. *Das Nachthorn* (The night watchman's horn) (Mönch von Salzburg)
With three different descant parts, the third in free paraphonia.

Zart-lieb-ste Frau in lie - ber Acht,wünsch mir ein lieb-lich fröhlich Nacht! Wenn

so mein Herz Dein Treu be-tracht', das freu - et all' mein Kraft und Macht auf

52

Schlaf be - kränk' weil ich die Nacht gar viel an Dich ge - denk. Süß'

Träum die ma - chen mir so heiß, daß ich mir eins nur weiß:

Daß ich schla - fen könnt ohn' Stra - fen in sol - cher lie - ber Sach ohn'

End!

55

13. *Recitative*
   In the episodes the third of each underlying chord, in decorated form, provides a melody over the paraphonic foundation.

14. *Pentatonic improvisation*

Over the three-part ostinato (2 players) that can last as long as desired and that should make a long crescendo and decrescendo, free melodic lines can be improvised. These can be shorter or longer, they can arise individually or they can overlap or build question and answer phrases. The ostinato can also be played alone. The accompanying parts come to an end in the reverse order to that in which they started.

When several players improvise it is important that each part is different from the other in character. Where one part is legato and sustained another should have more movement.

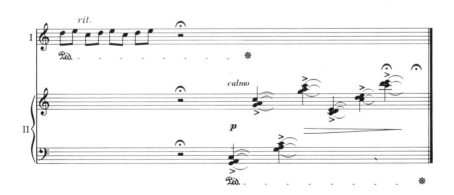

15. Study (compare ''Carl Orff und sein Werk,'' Vol. I, p. 301-312) Mirrored thirds, sixths and octaves.

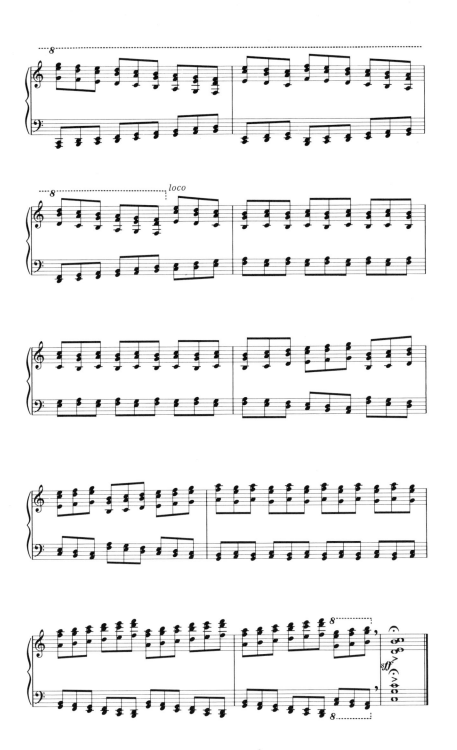

SCHOOL PERFORMANCES

We were always organising open evenings in smaller and larger halls to test our work, submit it to proof, and to make it more widely known. If on these first evenings gymnastic exercises were used as introductory material, these soon gave way to dance and music pieces, since public interest had shifted to this particular aspect of the work of the school.

Quite soon the particularly gifted students formed a small dance group; but we still lacked a really leading personality for teaching dance, so that the dances they made were usually in the convention of the times with choreography and mime mostly in the foreground.

A cross-section of the programme for the first three years will give a picture of our work. Besides dancing to piano pieces by Rameau there were also dances from his "Zoroastre". The "Dances from lute music of the sixteenth century" played by Anna Barbara Speckner on the harpsichord in her own arrangements had a special note in the programme. Among contemporary music we mostly used Bartók's piano pieces "For Children" — free arrangements of Hungarian and Slovakian folk tunes, and his famous "Allegro barbaro" — just made for dance. We also danced many versions of Stravinsky's "Pièces faciles" and Casella's "Pezzi infantili", all of it music suitable for movement.

The piano improvisations always created a small sensation in our performances at that time. Improvisations over broadly spaced out drones were made on two grand pianos using two, three or sometimes four players. Beside the malagueña, berceuses were especially popular. To prove the spontaneity of the improvisation partners exchanged roles and the pieces were played in many different ways. Descanting was mostly achieved with a convincing and easy fluidity. If someone did run off the rails this was only a further proof of the genuineness of the improvisation.

We were soon able to form a choir with the ever-growing number of students. Choral singing was included in my plan for music education as an essential element.

63

Once again I was lucky in getting Karl Marx, a former pupil who understood my work, to join our staff. He had become an experienced choral director and looked for material that would be suitable for us. Among other works, he arranged for us a series of old French Chansons that we performed frequently. We were soon able to include items in which the choir sang and danced simultaneously.

One that we used often was Karl Marx's setting of "Dans les jardins d'mon père".

        Et ma joli' colombe
        Qui chante jour et nuit,
        Qui chante pour les filles
        Qui n'ont point de mari!
Refrain: Auprès de ma blonde
           Qu'il fait bon, fait bon, fait bon!
           Auprès de ma blonde
           Qu'il fait bon dormir!

Dites-moi donc, la belle,
Où donc est vot' mari?
Il est dans la Hollande,
Les Hollandias l'ont pris.
Refrain: . . .

Que donneriez-vous, belle,
Pour avoir un ami?
Je donnerais Versailles,
Paris et Saint Denis!
Refrain: . . .

Je donnerais Versailles,
Paris et Saint Denis,
Les tours de Notre Dame,
Et l'clocher d'not' pays!
Refrain: . . .

Les tours de Notre Dame,
Et l'clocher d' not' pays,
Et ma joli' columbe,
Pour avoir un ami!
Refrain: . . .

It was interesting to observe how the qualities of the different languages, here the French, were expressed in the movement.

Mimed contributions also played a special role. Günther had already given classes in movement notation, choreography, mime, the study of costume and mask-making. For the first attempt at mime I found the "Tre Ciechi" (The Three Blind Men) from the little "Mascherata" (Masquerade) by Giovanni Domenico da Nola. The Three Blind Men provided perfect material for an attractive dance trio to which the choir sang as "onlookers".

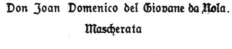

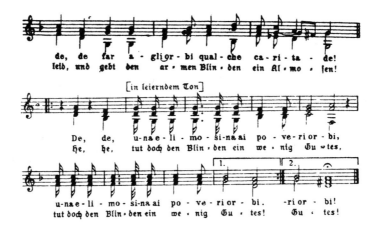

de, de far a - gli or - bi qual - che ca - ri - ta - de!
leib, und gebt den ar - men Blin - den ein Al - mo - fen!

[in leierndem Ton]

De, de, u - na e - li - mo - si - na ai po - ve - ri or - bi,
he, he, tut doch den Blin - den ein we - nig Gu - tes,

u - na e - li - mo - si - na ai po - ve - ri or - bi. -ri or - bi!
tut doch den Blin - den ein we - nig Gu - tes! Gu - tes!

I also sketched a small choreographic study that Günther worked
out in detail: "Dance of the Pages".

Five pages in five scenes presented a ceremonial dance around their
unseen mistress. I found suitable music in Samuel Scheidt's (1587 -
1654) "Passamezzo Variations" that Anna Barbara Speckner played
on the harpsichord. These delicate dances had the atmosphere of a
poem by Rainer Maria Rilke and one of them, a dance with moving
lights, remains particularly in my memory.

It was part of my plan to give improvisational tasks to the newly
formed choir as well. Pentatonic scales without semitones that can
form no dissonances also proved themselves particularly suitable
for the beginning. Our previous experiences with the piano
exercises stood us in good stead.

The choir director undertook the overall shape and the dynamic
structure. The results that often developed, particularly through
several repetitions, seemed to create a kind of magical effect that
communicated itself to the audience, when one was present, and
had its effect upon them. This technique produced such a strong
desire to imitate it that at the end of a school performance I was also
able to direct a group choral improvisation with the audience.

NEW COLLEAGUES

In 1925 and 1926 two students came to the school who, in the time of expansion that followed, were instrumental in its development and who gave equally to both the dance and the music a new, unmistakeable profile.

Maja Lex the dancer, born a dancer and for her entire life dedicated to dance as her element, found in the conditions at the school the ideal prerequisites for developing and bringing to maturity her talent, that was as considerable in music as it was in dance. As choreographer she found here her entirely personal style, that she was later able to unfold fully in the elemental dances she composed for the Güntherschule Dance Group that was founded in 1930.

Gunild Keetman, with her natural talent in equal parts for movement as for music, and who came to the school soon after Lex, became after a short time my helper and colleague in the further expansion of the musical training. It was to her that I gave the task of trying out the different playing techniques of the newly-developed barred instruments. It was she, who sketched out the first pieces for these instruments. I am not exaggerating when I say that without Keetman's decisive contribution through her double talent, "Schulwerk" could never have come into being.

It was Keetman too, who in her work with Maja Lex — a unique constellation — sketched out all the accompanying music to all the solo and group dances composed by Lex. Her no less important contribution to the international fame and success of the dance group through the dance orchestra, that she formed with the students and directed herself, was decisive.

THE PERCUSSION INSTRUMENTS

The group of instruments called percussion instruments, in which by tradition the timpani are not included, were first introduced in larger numbers into our western orchestras in the early decades of the 20th century.

Even though Mozart used bass drum, cymbal and triangle in his Janissary music in "Il Seraglio", and Beethoven used the same instruments in his Ninth Symphony, a row of percussion instruments is first seen (apart from a few exceptions in the Baroque period) in the scores of the Romantic and late Romantic period, particularly in those of Berlioz. They were included mostly for special effects in the ever larger orchestras.

In the "Traité d'instrumentation" of F. A. Gevaert, so famous in his day, we find in the chapter "The Percussion Instruments of Modern Music" the following sentences:

"From the two constituent elements of the essence of music, pitch and rhythm, these instruments generate only the second and subsidiary (!) element; in the hierarchy of musical instruments they therefore take the lowest rank. They also appear in works of art as occasional adjuncts for isolated moments." This was written and published in Paris 16 years after Berlioz' death!

In the huge score of his "Ring" Wagner merely uses 4 timpani, triangle, cymbals, tam-tam, tenor drum and glockenspiel, while Strauss in his "Salome" uses even 5 timpani, tam-tam, cymbals, bass and side drums, triangle, xylophone, castanets, glockenspiel and celeste, and in later scores demands even more instruments of this kind. In addition, in several cases, with Stravinsky, Bartók and others, the piano is used as a percussion instrument and is played in new ways and with new techniques.

As an independent group of instruments like a group of wind or string instruments, the percussion group first came into its own with the decisive change in styles of composition, with the beginning of the "New music" where it plays a partly leading and determinant role.

For my idea of developing an elemental music style the percussion instruments, whose origins stretch back to earliest antiquity, had the most decisive significance. They appeared here not accidentally but fundamentally, shaping form and tone colour, developing a life of their own.

In 1925 the instrument firm of Spangenberg in Dresden brought out a new kind of drum they had developed which they called a "kleine Tanzpauke" (a small dance timpani). Hindemith used them in his violin concerto and in his opera "Cardillac" and described them as "stimmbare Trommeln" (tunable drums). Mary Wigman included them in the accompaniments for her dance ensemble. It was there that I came to know these instruments. The name chosen by Spangenberg, "dance timpani" is misleading, since they are not real timpani having no "kettle" but being rather a single-skinned, cylindrical, tunable drum made in four sizes with approximately this range:

These dance timpani formed the basis of our percussion orchestra. A prospectus from the firm of Spangenberg will show the abundance of new instruments that were already available to us.

Through receiving various bequests we were able in a relatively short time to build up an orchestra as follows:

2 timpani
4 dance timpani
1 bass drum
some tenor drums
4 Chinese tom-toms in various sizes
1 Chinese barrel-shaped drum (most suitable for solos)
1 double-skinned cylindrical drum (used as a hand drum in various
   ways)
1 tambourine
several wood blocks
castanets
triangle
glockenspiel
4 large cymbals
1 large tam-tam and several smaller ones

The tambours were included only occasionally as a choir, but continued to have further use in the gymnastic lessons.

Individual timpani lessons were taken over by my former pupil and friend, Karl List, conductor at the Bayerische Rundfunk (Bavarian Radio) and originally a timpanist. He was also able to give instruction on how to play the other more important instruments, in particular the tam-tam, the different drums, cymbal and glockenspiel. A special time was set aside for this since proper professional instruction and supervised practice were absolutely necessary.

Our work with our now extended percussion ensemble formed a seamless unity with our rhythmic exercises with clapping and stamping, with rattles and drums, or — in fact rather developed from it. Of course we spent hours and hours experimenting with the new instruments, the different ways of striking and playing them, and the different ways in which they could be used — we were orchestrating.

While we were spending much time in working out the rhythmic examples I wanted at the same time to pursue the study of tone colour.

In an old chrestomathy, a collection of the earliest poetry, I found a German translation by Johann Gottfried Herder of a Latin poem. The Roman Emperor Hadrian (76 - 138) is supposed to have written it shortly before his death. Herder gives it the title: "Sterbelied an seine Seele" (Death Song to His Soul). I managed to find the original text and was very affected by its unusual quality. It was verse that rang like music. For a long time I had wanted to try a study for tam-tam alone, and here I found the opportunity of beginning the verse with a kind of oath: with soft "invocations" on the tam-tam, freely declaimed in speech rhythm, as we had already tried in a different context on the drum.

> Animula vagula blandula,
> hospes comesque corporis,
> quae nunc abibis in loca
> pallidula rigida nudula
> nec ut soles dabis jocos.

> Little soul, vagrant, attractive,
> My body's guest and companion.
> Now you will vanish to a place,
> Pale, rigid, bare,
> And all alone your jokes are over.

"Rulers are distinguished by their deeds. Only a few were able to show publicly their common humanity. In Hadrian's Animula poem the human being transcends the emperor, and both are transcended by the poet Hadrian, who was allowed in a few lines to make the atmosphere of the death of his mortal soul immortal." (German translation and text by Josef Fink)

A successful recitation could produce a breathless tension. The dialogue with the tam-tam gives resonance to something beyond the power of words to describe. Someone who had made such an attempt will come nearer to understanding the secret of this instrument. We were continually trying to find new ways of interpreting this text.

Ad me ipsum

Tamtam vom Sprecher geschlagen,
in langsamen, freien Sprechtempo.

♩. sempre pp, molto rubato con estrema sensibilità

Tamtam

animu-la va-gula blandula,

hospes comesque corpo-ris,

quae nunc abi-bis in lo-ca

palli-dula ri-gida nudu-la

nec ut soles dabis io-cos.

Tamtam

langsamer.

Our friend Lang, on his excursions to the antique shops in Schwabing and to the booths at second-hand fairs and sales, was always purchasing exotica for us in the form of new, and to us valuable instruments: unusual rattles, little bells and on one occasion a larger African slit drum. Such acquisitions were always an inducement for study and discovery in the field of tone colour. In this way new experiments came into being, sometimes without text. One of these had the title "Fear".

A quiet, continuous roll on a muffled bass drum, to which two alternating wood blocks are added, giving absolutely regular beats like the ticking of a clock. On the slit drum quiet, throbbing beats like some fantastic morse code, and always interspersed with rests. Over this ostinato, very gradually, fleeting sounds are heard — with wire brush, soft and hard beaters on timpani and drum, with a triangle beater striking a hanging cymbal in the greatest variety of places and producing a "ringing lights" effect, with the excitement of playing with "thimbled" fingers on tom-toms, with bamboo sticks and with wood scraps. The labyrinth of indefinable sounds becomes more and more dense, flowing over and under one another, imitating and mirroring, not fixable in a score, arising and dissolving differently every time, exciting and therefore corresponding to the idea and imaginative picture of the theme. Everything increases until the beats on the wood blocks stop suddenly and there is an immediate silence. After a moment the slit drum recommences with even, crescendoing beats, joined by all the other instruments one by one till a loud cymbal clash indicates the end. Another rest — a quiet, resonant beat on the tam-tam.

We tried this many times and it was always different. With satisfaction I could establish that the ability to make music in this way came from our previous experience with the rhythmic exercises and without these it would have been unthinkable. The new varieties of tone colour tempted us to create these "nocturnal scenes" (the "nocturnal" was there, but not verbalised). We never tried anything similar again. Instead movement and dance, that were still lacking at that time, came more and more into the foreground.

CONDUCTING EXERCISES

Our experiments with tone colour pieces had proved to be a really interesting period, necessary for development if not without its dangers — how quickly each effect wears out. Once this period came to an end we began with new forms of improvisation, that particularly stressed architectural structure as well as tone colour.

We had made and tried out our pieces working and "playing" together. Now *one* person should take over the direction and development while the others subordinated and adapted themselves to her ideas.

The conducting exercises that arose out of this had little to do with the usual conducting of music that is written down and supplied to both players and conductor. It was not beating time, nor did it give the time structure, but it was the forming of an improvisation through gesture. Of course time structures and the relevant techniques were practised; whereupon it came to me that this was almost a dance-like direction of music that was in many ways improvised, as was the case with all our exercises so far. The music came out according to the movement.

Certain rhythms were indicated by the conductor through unmistakeable signs. Every beat, every rhythm was presented through gesture, and this included dynamics and tempo. Each instrument or group of instruments was directly addressed and led. There were special signs for the maintaining of an ostinato and for stopping. Sometimes the rhythm was quite free, we would call it aleatory today, and this, too, was indicated by gesture. The exercise presented a double improvisation task: for the conductor who must shape every aspect of the music's structure, and for the players who could fill out certain parts of the given form with their own improvisations.

Apart from conducting improvisations that were quite free and that also sometimes had themes such as "Riot", "Procession", "Waves on the sea", "Litany", and so on, we depended particularly on the rhythms of the old dance forms. Next to processional pieces we dared to present grandiose galliards and pavanes, sarabandes with solemn tam-tam, moresques with tambourine and castanets, forms that repeatedly invited new settings.

74

Even though very varied architecturally, these studies were no more than rhythmic skeletons. The leading role of a melody and an accompaniment that fitted it in tone colour were missing. We had been able to prepare both in our piano improvisations. If we wished to transfer what we had learned there onto our orchestra as it was at present, it was clear that we were lacking the necessary instruments.

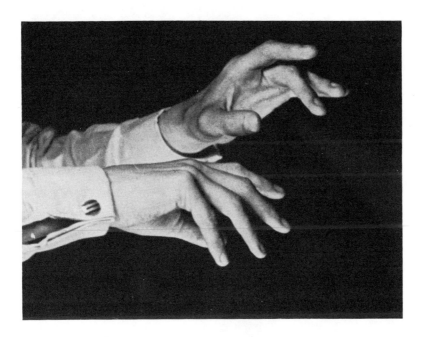

First exercises

Entry

Piano

Crescendo

Down-beat

Conductor . . . .

. . . and group

Entry with cymbal clash

Pavane

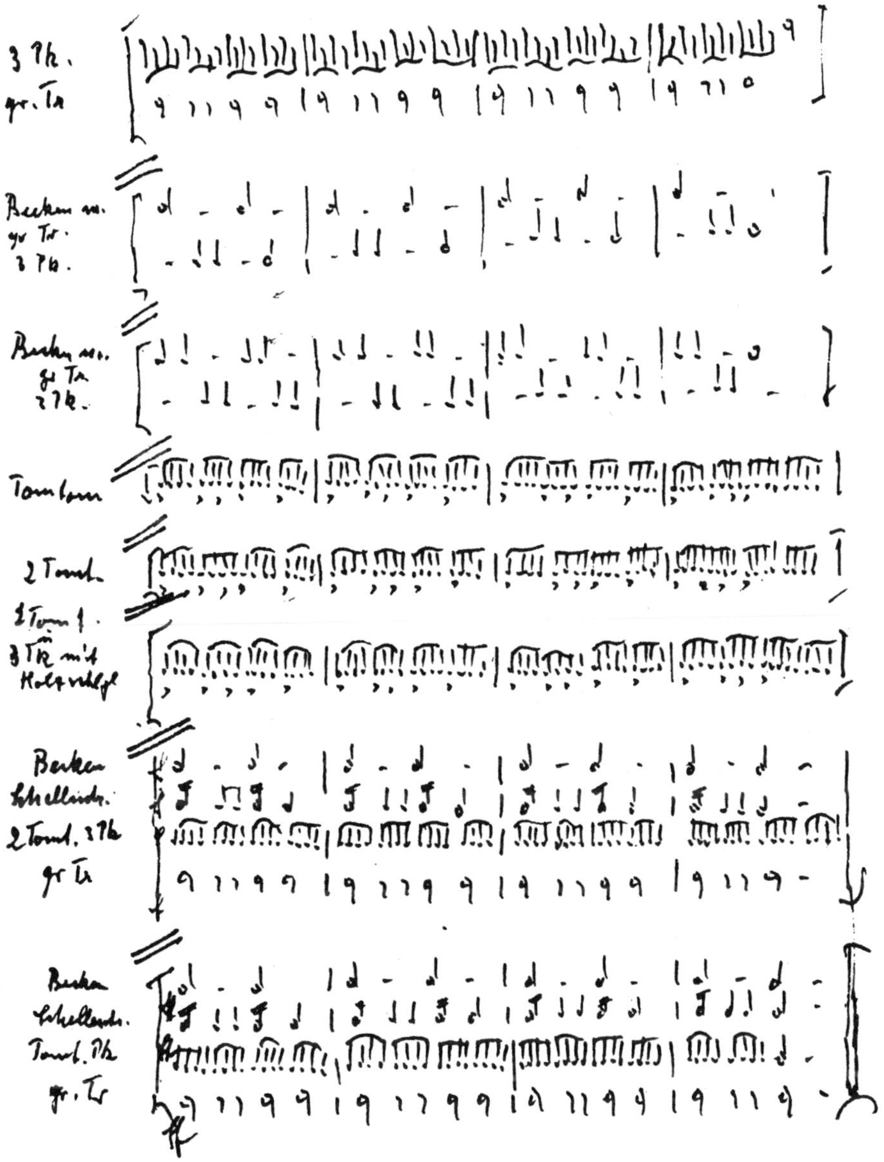

Sarabande

+ Schlag auf Beckenkuppe.

Moresca

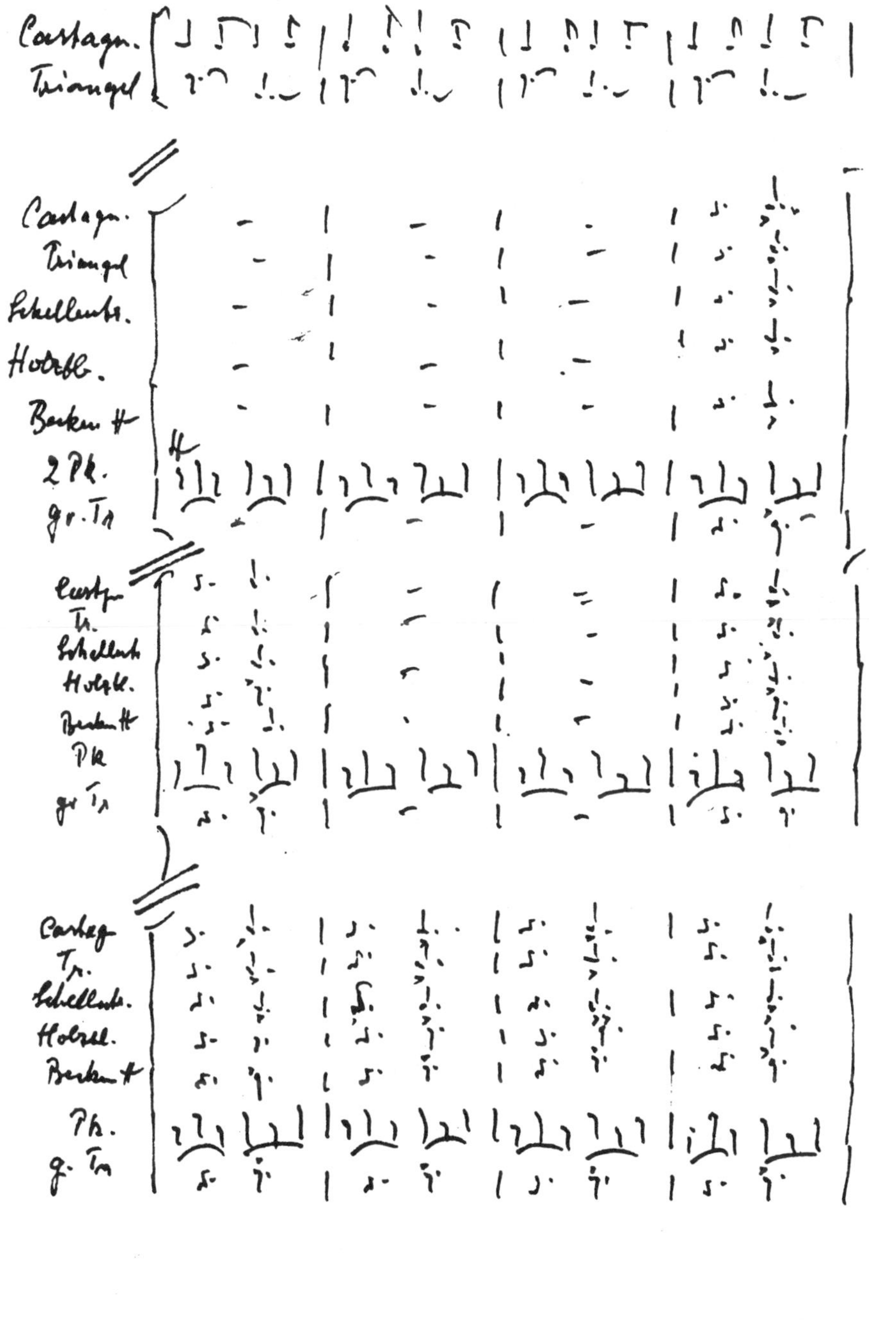
Castagn.
Triangel
Castagn.
Triangel
Holzbl.
2 Pk.
Pk
Pk.

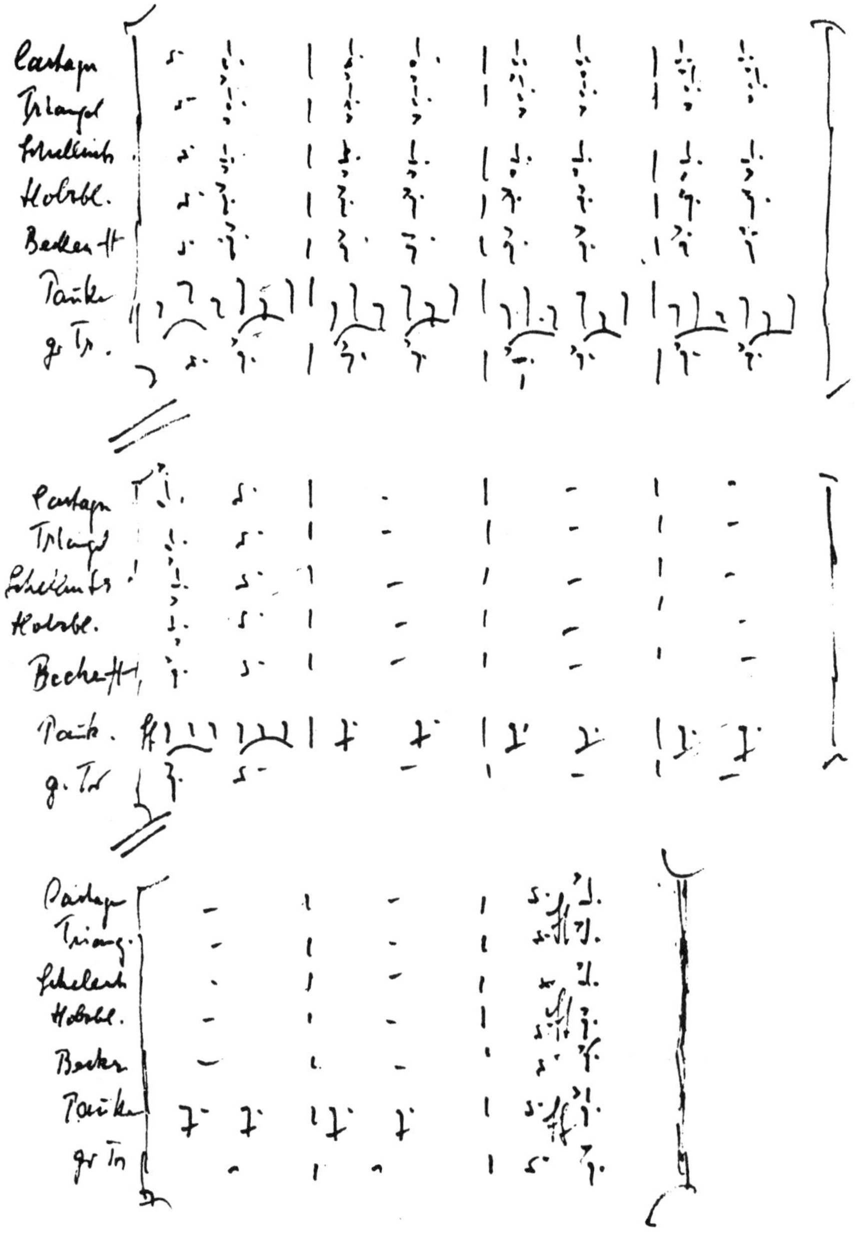
Holzbl.
Pauke
gr. Tr.

SOMETHING NEW IN VIEW

Autumn 1926. Oskar Lang was once again visiting us in the school. The percussion improvisations and the conducting lessons interested him very much. As usual we had a long discussion that gave me a series of new ideas. Finally Lang asked if he could bring along some friends who would have a special understanding for my work.

So one day he came with two Swedish sisters. They worked with puppets and were interested in my musical experiments, about which they had heard from Lang. The way they reacted to my work attracted my attention, so that when they invited me to visit them and see their work, I readily accepted.

In deepest Schwabing, in the small, out of the way Wagnerstrasse, in a large, old, already dilapidated studio a little theatre had been built. Everything was still *in statu nascendi* but one could imagine what the sisters had in mind. The whole undertaking, from the hand-carved puppets to the way the scenery was arranged was absolutely novel, full of imagination, and in it's way convincing. The only essential thing that was lacking was suitable music, and this they had not yet found. A friend's attempts at an improvised accompaniment on a violin were touching but somewhat helpless. Now that they had seen and heard our percussion ensemble they were full of new plans. It was also clear to me that a collaboration with the sisters might produce some interesting results.

After an improvised performance of a Flemish legend and scenes from Strindberg's fairy tale "Swanwhite" we had a long talk and I discovered how widely travelled and well-informed the Swedish sisters were. It was inevitable that we should talk of the great eastern originals. They had witnessed both Chinese and Javanese shadow plays with their unusual small orchestras and had many excellent photographs.

They were also able to talk about Gamelan orchestras and felt that the xylophone was particularly appropriate for the puppet theatre. I listened attentively and was reminded of my earlier attempts with a puppet theatre, when I enacted Maeterlinck's "Death of Tintagiles" and of how a small Chinese drum was the source of inspiration for a whole scene. I already saw a small percussion orchestra, different from the one we had in the school, a chamber music ensemble with a xylophone that would suit the puppets so well. The sisters were thrilled with this idea. We were all — Lang was there — indulging in fantasies and plans. It was by no means a wasted evening.

I left the unusual studio with its charming sisters with the promise that I would return soon and perhaps bring with me a small group of percussion players from the school. The sisters promised that through their Oriental connections they would try to procure for me a Gamelan xylophone. I was touched by their kindness but did not hold out too much hope that they would be successful.

Lang and I went on to a café and stayed till after midnight talking in the same vein and thinking of how Stravinsky, after the war, wanted to get together a travelling company of actors and musicians. "The Soldier's Tale" came from this idea. A travelling puppet theatre like the one I had known as a child, but with a new kind of music, perhaps even improvised — this thought took root in my mind.

After a few weeks a parcel arrived for me at the school. To my absolute astonishment it contained a large African xylophone, a marimba such as those I had seen in collections but had never had the opportunity to play, let alone the hope of possessing. The only clue to the sender was a note inside — "Greetings from Africa. Lycka till!" (Swedish for "Good luck!")

I asked Lang at once for the telephone number of the Swedish sisters. He told me that the elder one had become seriously ill and they had both returned home leaving no address. In spite of many efforts to find them I never heard from them again.

BARRED INSTRUMENTS AND RECORDERS

So the marimba had come to me in the school.

For hours I let my imagination play and improvised on the new African xylophone, trying out every possible way of playing and striking it with different kinds of beaters; long quiet tremolos, using two beaters in each hand, single and double glissandi. A whole new world of sound had opened up for me and I was fascinated.

At one stroke I had found what I needed for the further extension of my educational ideas and for the dance orchestra, an instrument that would supply those resonances that had previously been missing and upon which melodies and ostinati of all kinds could be built. As I looked back at the earlier percussion experiments they seemed to me like incomplete, skeletonal sketches that could only now be meaningfully performed.

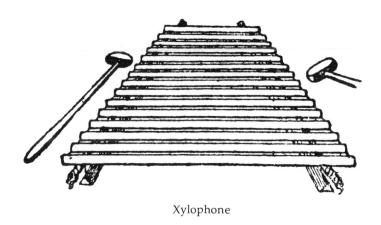

Xylophone

The origins of the xylophone go back to the earliest times. Coming originally from South East Asia, Melanesia and Indonesia where primitive forms gave way to those with trough or box resonators, it arose later in Africa as a marimba with its own special forms and from there, through the negro slaves, it reached Latin America where it became indigenous to the folk music.

The name xylophone appears to have been used in Europe from the beginning of the nineteenth century for an instrument that had been used in folk music throughout Slavonic and German-speaking countries since the Middle Ages. It was surely introduced in primitive forms into German speaking regions by means of travelling musicians from the Far East in about the fifteenth century.

"Hülzern Glachter"

Since the sixteenth century one meets the folk name "Hülzern Glachter" derived from the dialect forms of the German for "wood" and for "mallet". Other names to be found include "Holzharmonika", "Holzfidel" or "Strohfidel".

In contrast to the non-European xylophone its development in Europe was limited. Not until the nineteenth century did it make a temporary appearance as an orchestral instrument in a version called a four-row xylophone.

In "Salome" Richard Strauss describes the xylophone as a "Holz- und Strohinstrument". This describes the way it was then built, for the wooden bars were placed upon bales of straw (Stroh). This name and form have long since disappeared.

90

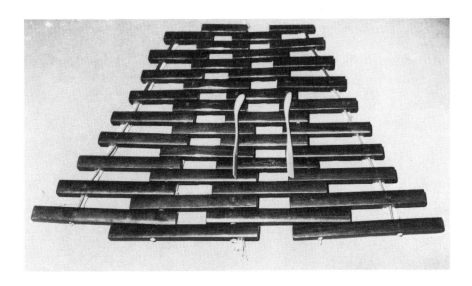

Four-row orchestral xylophone

The American model, with its piano keyboard arrangement and with its tone amplification by means of individual resonators, has taken its place in more recent times. For the time being the development of the western form of the xylophone has reached a conclusive stage.

American model

In 1889 Debussy came into contact with the music of the Far East through the World Exhibition in Paris. This contact was of great significance to his artistic development. He had come under the spell of the colourful and unique sound of Gamelan music.

"For days on end he listened with his friends to the exotic orchestras and theatres that China, India and Java had sent to Paris . . .

"If any music can be said to have 'influenced' Debussy, then it is the swaying, form free, gentle music of the Far East. It comes nearer to the character of his own music than does the whole of the music of nineteenth century Europe. In comparison with the refined and blended sound of this orchestra the percussion instruments of the cultured European orchestra only produced the barbaric noise of the circus — this is the impression of the young composer that he endorsed with the authority of a master five years before his death." (Heinrich Strobel "Claude Debussy")

The Gamelan music of Indonesia, with its polyrhythms and polyphony can be considered as the peak of achievement for a non-European music culture, and is from a certain viewpoint an equal counterpart to western art music, looking back as it does over hundreds of years' history. Even when only considered visually, this orchestra from the East, with its instruments that have a cultish and magical meaning, leaves behind an overwhelming impression.

In spite of the profound and directional influence of the sound of the Gamelan orchestra upon Debussy, he never used such an instrument in any of his works.

The instruments of an Indonesian Gamelan Orchestra

93

For me an experience no less weighty was intended. It was the sound of one single instrument, the marimba. —

Marimba from the Cameroons

This one instrument initiated not only a new stage in my educational work but also provided an important point of departure for all my subsequent compositions.

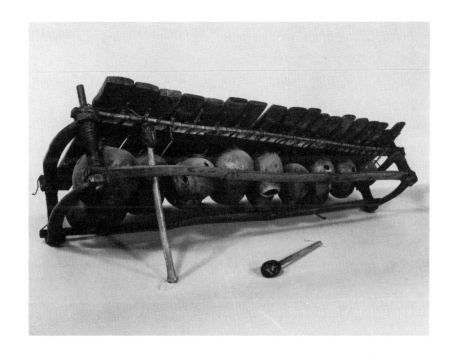

Marimba from Central Africa

I asked Keetman to familiarise herself with the technique of playing the new instrument, whose African tuning contained intervals that were smaller than a semitone and that would be difficult to combine with our western tuning.

As Keetman practised after the school day and far into the night — we liked best to play the marimba four-handed, not knowing that this was quite usual in its home country — it arose quite naturally that more and more of the students came to listen, and that they brought with them a variety of small percussion instruments such as rattles, jingles and drums. Out of the first tentative improvisation experiments they soon achieved a real ensemble.

Lex was also drawn into these evenings and her delight in the new sounds inspired her to compose a dance study "Stäbetanz" (the dance of the marimba bars).

Attractive as all these experiments were, it was clear that an instrument that fitted into our western tuning would have to be made. For advice about this I went once more to Curt Sachs who had so many examples of this kind of instrument to hand.

He advised me strongly against trying to reproduce the African models that existed in different tunings. Their construction was of purely African origin. The materials (the right kind of wood for the bars and the calabash resonators) were not available. Even if one had success with the making of *one* instrument, the making of a series of them was unthinkable.

"You should use recorders, then you will have what you most need, a melody instrument to your percussion, the pipe to the drum, corresponding to historical development."

I had already thought of this kind of wind instrument, but there are as many different kinds as there are drums. Sachs thought that only the recorder should come into consideration. I knew these instruments from amateur circles that gave themselves to the playing of baroque music, and I had heard of Arnold Dolmetsch in Haslemere, England, who made excellent recorders and who was dedicated to the performance of baroque music on newly made "old instruments".

In spite of a high esteem for the outstanding musicological research that established a style of playing, I was following other paths. I also did not wish to appear to have any parallel relationship to Fritz Jöde's efforts at introducing the recorder to the youth movement in the Germany of the early twenties.

Sachs understood my objections but was able to refute them historically by suggesting that the baroque way of playing the recorder had by no means exhausted all possibilities, and that other sound qualities could be produced with a different blowing technique.

When, finally, he told me that some old forms of recorders (bone flutes) that could be dated as having belonged to the Stone Age had been found in northern Europe, I felt freed of all misgivings at the idea of including an avowed baroque art instrument in my elemental music ensemble.

At the same time he advised me to approach his friend Peter Harlan who had a workshop in Markneukirchen where he made lutes, viols and above all recorders. Sachs thought he would be the right person with his roots in history but open to all new techniques.

Above all I was fascinated with the idea of including a quartet of recorders: soprano (descant), alto (treble), tenor and bass, in my instrumental ensemble. The fact that these instruments were not too difficult to play was an advantage that was not to be overlooked. While still in Berlin, with a covering letter of recommendation from Sachs, I ordered from Harlan a full set of recorders, and the thought of them kindled once more the fire of my lively imagination.

And so I returned to Munich with one hope gone — I could not yet get over my xylophone dream — but with a new one growing as I thought of the recorders.

When I came to school the following morning, they were all so convinced that my Berlin visit had been a success as usual, that I was able to ignore the pertinent questions. Lex and Keetman showed me the beginning of the now finished "Stäbetanz" that I had not yet seen. In the shortest time they had rehearsed and produced it. Seldom have I been more convinced of the way in which music can evoke movement, and movement, music. The marimba, played four-handed, created a minor sensation with the way it fitted in with the small ensemble of glockenspiel, tom-tom, tambourine and jingles, in spite of its different tuning.

Stäbetanz, accompanied by marimba, played four-handed, and small percussion

STÄBETANZ

The first pages of the score in Keetman's handwriting

100

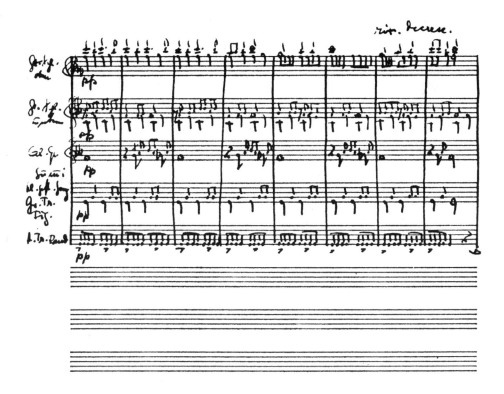

I found it rather hard to have to break the news of my discussion with Sachs that was, after all, partly negative. I tried to overcome the general disappointment over our misfired hopes and expectations by presenting the attraction of the new recorder plans with conviction. Following a unanimous decision that everyone should learn recorder, the introduction of this subject into the curriculum was a foregone conclusion. A new wave of enthusiasm swept through the school.

While we waited with excitement for the arrival of the recorders, a surprise for all of us arrived in the shape of a crate from Hamburg. It had been sent by one of our students and contained a "Kaffir piano" that had been sold privately in the port by a sailor who had just come from the Cameroons. The resonance box of this Kaffir piano, a crude name for a simple African xylophone, consisted of an ordinary wooden box that one might have found in any builder's yard and that had once contained builder's nails and still bore the burnt-on German lettering "10 000 Bretterstifte".

"Kaffir piano"

The only African things about this xylophone were the wooden bars of palisander, strung by means of laces across the open side of the box, thus providing an example of a primitive form of box or trough xylophone without any kind of resonator.

When struck with suitable beaters this xylophone produced a beautiful, full tone similar to the marimba, and its tuning was nearer to European pitch so that it could therefore be used immediately.

Keetman had soon written a book with some pieces for this xylophone in combination with other percussion instruments. Parts were copied out and passed from hand to hand. Hourly, daily and for half the night the instrument was used for practice, rehearsal and play, both two-handed and four-handed.

Sach's misgivings about the reproduction of xylophones could not possibly apply to this African model of unsurpassed simplicity and almost a product of chance, and it should be possible to produce such a simple box without resonators.

For this purpose I turned to my friend Karl Maendler, an inventive restorer of the craft of building harpsichords, and a talented maker of big, new concert harpsichords, that according to the practice of the times were used in large numbers and in large halls.

Together with Pleyel and Erard his name cannot be excluded from the history of harpsichord making. In addition, as with most inventors, he was an enthusiastic amateur constructor, and as such a man after my own heart. In all my earlier experiments at making new settings of old masters, be it Monteverdi or another, he had stood by my side and given advice. I had spent many long evenings and half nights in his unique workshop, playing the harpsichord and engaging in all sorts of experiments. For me there was no doubt: Maendler was the man who could help me this time.

So I invited him, since he was not only interested in music but also in movement, to an improvised performance. Of course we showed him the "Stäbetanz" first. He would not have been Maendler if the

103

sound of our marimba had not fascinated him. He understood at once what I wanted of him.

One performance was not enough for him. After the third he said he was racking his brains over the marimba; for he was sure that we were going to expect him to build such a marimba for us.

Now Keetman brought in the "Kaffir piano" and played on it, solo pieces at first and then with additional improvised percussion. He hoped that he could build *such* an instrument but only asked that it should not be called a "Kaffir piano".

The ice was broken — and one evening Maendler brought us his xylophone. Keetman and some of the students were still in the school and we immediately produced an improvised concert. Keetman had by now such a considerable experience of playing that she was able to introduce the instrument successfully.

The students were so enthusiastic that Maendler spontaneously promised to add to his first, an alto xylophone as he called it, a second one that would sound an octave higher and be called a soprano xylophone. Both these xylophones, because of the awaited recorders that we knew were to be made in D, had the following notes and range:

Soprano and alto xylophone with laced bars

104

Karl Maendler 1938

Later the notes on the alto and soprano xylophones were secured by means of nails so that notes could be interchanged and other keys formed, thus increasing the range of usefulness of the instrument.

Soprano and alto xylophones, the bars secured with nails

The building of a chromatic xylophone with 25 notes further enriched the possibilities of tone quality. Its range was

This time the new instrument had a noticeable relationship with eastern forms. Maendler made two models, one where the notes were suspended by means of laces over a cradle-shaped box, and the other where the notes were held in place by nails on a more rectangular box. Why he called these instruments "tenor xylophones" I can no longer remember.

Box xylophone in the shape of a cradle, with laced bars (Thailand)

Only on this instrument with its adjacent semitones was it possible to play effective glissandi that had a magical effect. Hard and soft beaters or even bamboo sticks were used.

107

Cradle-shaped
with laced bars

Tenor xylophones

Box-shaped
bars held with nails

Meanwhile the long-awaited recorders had come from Harlan. As we unpacked the parcels we looked in vain for a fingering chart or some form of playing instructions. We looked at our new instruments with some perplexity. At that time the famous "Traité de la Flute à bec" by Jacques Hotteterre, Paris 1728, was not available to us.

From the "Traité" of Hotteterre

List, to whom I turned for advice, said that within eight days he would be able to start giving lessons, although he had never concerned himself with recorders before. There was a recorder quartet in Munich at the time, four eccentric, elderly painters who played old music with enthusiasm on old, inherited instruments. As I learned later, it was from them that List acquired his first knowledge of these instruments. Keetman was different: "Give me a recorder and I will find out how it works — in a month the lessons will begin!" In this way Keetman experimented autodidactically and developed an individual, rhythmic-dynamically emphasised way of playing that fitted our music style.

"Medias in res" once more. We happily had our recorders and had taken the trouble to master the early stages of playing them. At the same time we used our meagre beginner's resources to improvise for movement, for dance. Two recorders started with drone and melody, an accompaniment on a double-skinned drum joined them and together they inspired the dance, which further stimulated the musicians. The following photographs were taken of these first attempts — untrammelled, elemental:

Improvisation on alto and tenor recorder . . .

. . . with double-skinned drum . . .

. . . to dance

112

113

FIRST PUBLICATIONS

1930. The time for experiments had come to a kind of conclusion. We had traversed our first field and a new one lay before us.

My two publisher friends, the brothers Ludwig and Willy Strecker, had often visited the school and were very interested in everything that had to do with a new attitude to music education. The improvisation and conducting exercises, the ensemble, dance and orchestral exercises never failed to have their effect. The charming girl students with their unencumbered youth also excited admiration, as adept at dancing as they were with an instrument.

In the summer of 1930 I was at the Music Festival of the "Allegemeinen Deutschen Musikvereins" in Königsberg where Scherchen had given the first performance of my Entrata. I took the opportunity of arranging a meeting there with Willy Strecker, to discuss with him the possibility of publishing my work and experiences at the Güntherschule. I had carried this idea around with me for some time but had so far come to no solution that was precise or practicable. It was clear to me that publication was inevitable and necessary if I wanted my work to be known to a wider public.

During a two-hour morning walk I laid out for Strecker my then revolutionary plans for a new music education, and, growing from them, a fundamental, general education, and I did not economise in grand, prophetic words.

Finally he said: "I find your ideas very interesting and well thought out; the problem is, how will you carry them out? I well understand that you need above all some published material. But are you not expecting rather a lot of your publisher? I should publish music for instruments that do not exist — apart from your few experimental and sample versions; I should propagate an approach to education for whom there are no teachers — apart from some of your students, and for which there is certainly very little understanding, and that will certainly meet much resistance from established professional groups. But I must admit that your idea is so fantastic that I will risk a couple of trial volumes."

Over a late breakfast, on the reverse side of the hotel bill, we worked out a contract which said that "the educational work, that is herewith given to the publisher" — there was no more talk of "trial" volumes — "shall carry the title "Orff-Schulwerk — Elementare Musikübung"."

Once more at home I began with feverish activity to work out all that I had sketched out to Willy Strecker on the spur of the moment. How carefree I had been, how optimistically I had recited my plans without the faintest idea of the lifelong adventure into which I was plunging!

I now endeavoured to put together a first book that would encompass the fundamentals. This had to come mostly from memory, from remembering some of my lessons, from chance sketches that I had made. I could go back to many of the rhythms and melodies that had been thought of and tried out in movement sessions, or that had resulted from the sessions themselves, arising out of and for that particular moment.

As I worked as a compiler so many ideas for further material were awakened in me that I was soon no longer collecting but rather selecting and sifting. Those who know my way of working will understand how it was that the collecting of material in itself continuously stimulated me to think of new ideas. That is why pieces can be found in the volumes that are borderline cases for composition, as so often happens when improvisations are written down in notation.

This random collection of rhythms and melodies with over 250 examples and models called "Rhythmisch-melodische Übung" opened the Orff-Schulwerk series of publications.

With the appearance of these volumes a new chapter in the history of Orff-Schulwerk was started. I knew that the publication and the attendant fixing in notation form did not correspond to the nature of improvisation, but it was unavoidable for the development and expansion of the work. One constraint was gone, one bond loosened.

RHYTHMISCH-MELODISCHE ÜBUNG

Extracts from the first edition of 1931

The examples can be varied: changes of dynamics, extension of form, set vocally, instrumentally, for solo or chorus, texts can be invented to fit and in particular they can be used for movement.

I.

1. Articulation and phrasing

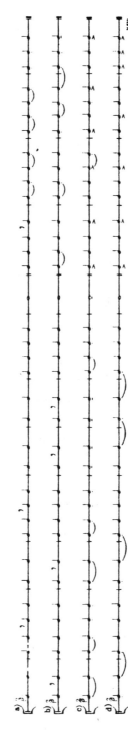

2. Making a melody from a given rhythm

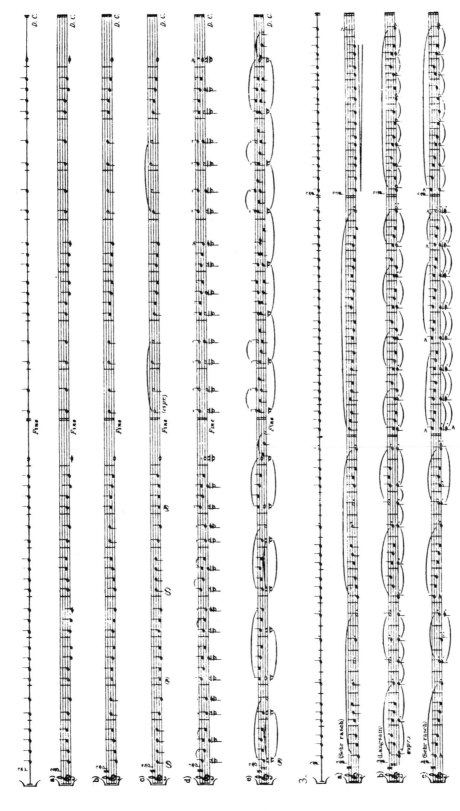

II.

Counting-out rhymes

118

III.

9. Freely-made rhythm over an ostinato accompaniment

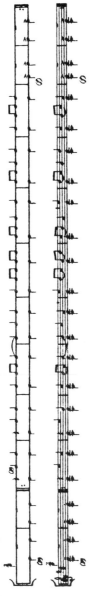

10. The same task with an additional bass part

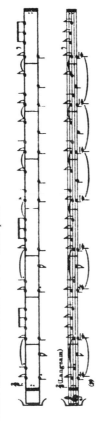

11. Freely made melody over given accompanying rhythm
(Rhythm is taken over by the middle part in the second half)

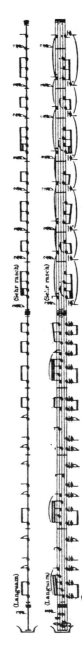

119

12.   Three-part clapping rhythm
      a) instrumental (2 wood blocks and castanets)

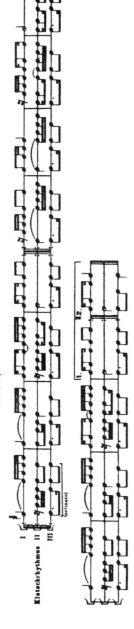

b) arranged vocally

13. A rhythmic accompaniment to a given melody

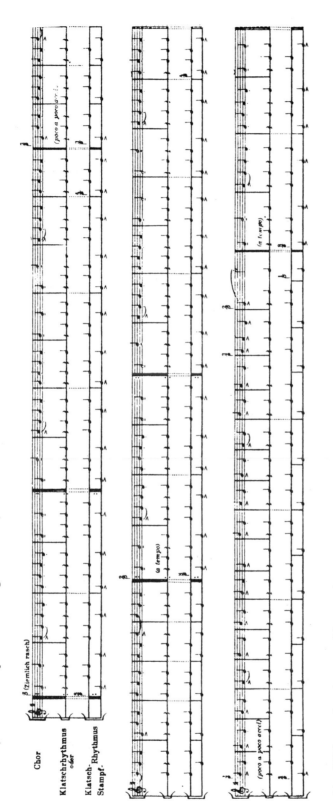

14. With moving drone and harmonic support

IV.

Choral and recorder ostinati with freely-made melody as an example for further improvisation

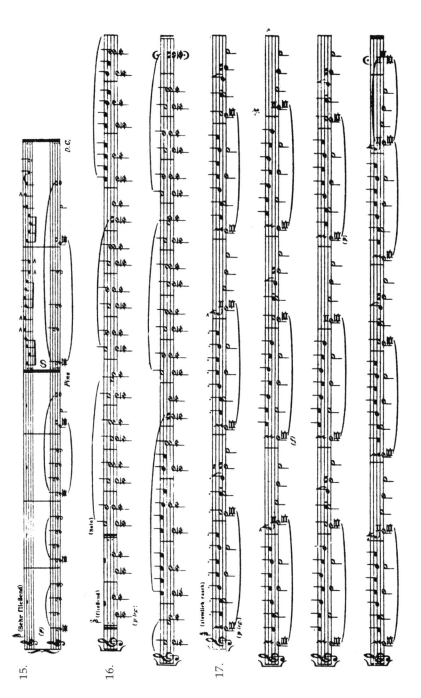

20. Freely-made further extension

Melodic studies

Rhythmic exercises with chorus of speakers

VII.

Three dance pieces to be sung to an accompaniment of clapping and stamping

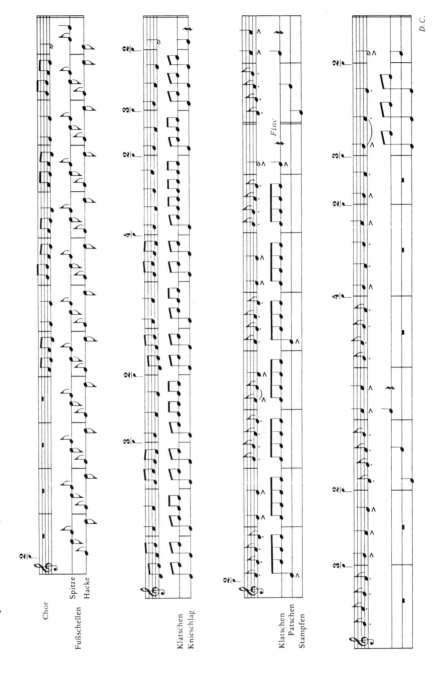

126

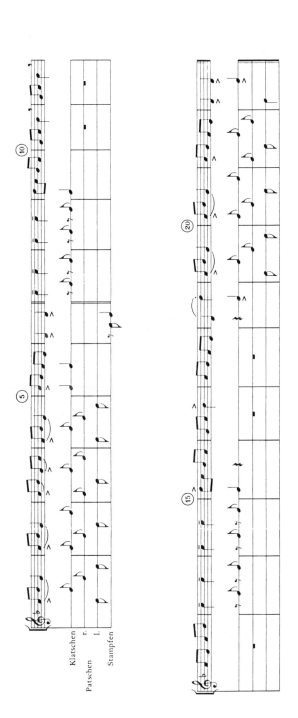

with freely-improvised clapping accompaniment

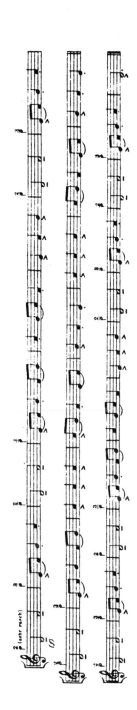

VIII.

Choral and instrumental exercises

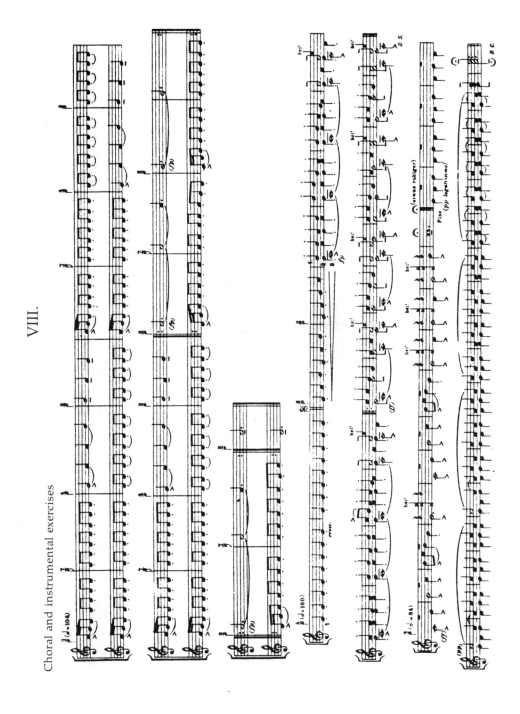

37.

For choir and instruments

38.

For glockenspiel, xylophone, small cymbal, large cymbal and timpani

39.

40. For wind instruments, barred percussion, timpani and small percussion

41. Tutti and a string bass instrument

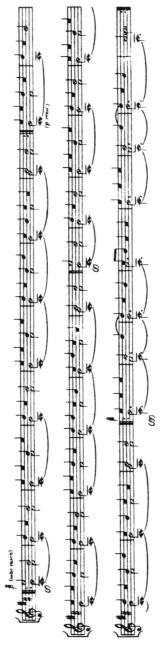

42. Tutti

130

Unfortunately the "Rhythmisch-melodische Übung", offering sample material as it did, was widely misunderstood, since it is possible to practise and perform each piece as it stands. To do this would mean a total failure to recognise the purpose of the book. It is not the playing from notation but the free making of music in improvisation that is meant and demanded, for which the printed examples give information and stimulus.

Spontaneous teaching that comes totally from improvisation is and remains an excellent starting point. Experience has nevertheless shown that not everyone is capable of teaching in this way; it can therefore not be expected from everyone.

It is a play of their imagination that can be achieved through the building-up of the most simple rhythms and melodies, drones and ostinati, with the inclusion of all possible kinds of instrument, and it is the imagination that should be awakened and trained by these means.

The time-consuming editing of the Schulwerk editions was now added to the burden of the ever-expanding number of students and therefore of lessons. This was all too much for me so that I had to look for an assistant. Once again I was helped by a lucky chance. Hans Bergese, a young music student from Freiburg im Breisgau, a pupil of Gurlitt, v. Ficker and Sachs, attended one of our holiday courses at the Musikheim in Frankfurt on the Oder. He felt himself immediately drawn to the work. I also felt that he was so suitable that, after a short period of study with me and at the school, I installed him as my assistant and later as my deputy, and immediately engaged him to help me with the production of the Schulwerk books.

In 1934 I was also able to gain the services of Dr. Wilhelm Twittenhoff at the Güntherschule. He was a music pedagogue who was much concerned with the youth movement. Twittenhoff also helped with the production of books and, within the framework of the whole series, he wrote an introduction that was published in 1935.

As well as the rhythmic-melodic exercises, some books were published with fully worked-out scores that presupposed a different kind of music-making. Examples of these were the books with exercises for hand drum, timpani, barred instruments and recorders.

The range of Schulwerk books published by Schott, Mainz, between 1931 and 1934:

ORFF-SCHULWERK

Elementare Musikübung

A	1	Rhythmisch-melodische Übung 1.u.2. Teil (Carl Orff)	1931
B	1	Übung für Schlagwerk: Handtrommel (Hans Bergese)	1931
B	2	Übung für Schlagwerk: Pauken (Hans Bergese)	1932
C	1	Stücke zum Singen und Spielen (Hans Bergese)	1933
D	1	Übung für Stabspiele: Xylophon (Hans Bergese)	1932
E	1	Spielstücke für kleines Schlagwerk (Hans Bergese)	1930
E	2	Spielstücke für kleines Schlagwerk (Gunild Keetman)	1931
F	1	Kleines Flötenbuch 1 (Gunild Keetman)	1934
F	2	Kleines Flötenbuch 2 (Gunild Keetman)	1934
G	1	Spielstücke für Blockflöte (Gunild Keetman)	1932
H	1	Spielstücke f. Blockflöten u. kl. Schlagwerk (Keetman)	1930
J	1	Tanz- und Spielstücke: Auftakt und Bolero (Keetman)	1930
J	2	Tanz (Keetman)	1930
J	3	Ekstatischer Tanz, Nachtlied (Keetman)	1932

In explanation of the above for the English reader: Übung = exercise; Schlagwerk = hand percussion; Handtrommel = hand drum, tambour; Pauken = timpani; Stücke = pieces; Spielen = playing; Stabspiele = barred percussion; kleines = small; Flötenbuch = recorder book; Blockflöte = recorder; Tanz = dance; Nachtlied = night song.

In 1933 some books came out with piano and violin exercises ("Klavierübung" and "Geigenübung"). They mostly contained transcriptions from the rhythmic-melodic exercises and from the other Schulwerk books. They were meant to show how fundamental the rhythmic-melodic exercises were and how they could correspondingly be further used and expanded. The only additional book that could be published in 1938 was the separate book "Alte und Neue Tänze für Blockflöte und Handtrommel" (Old and new dances for recorder and hand drum) by Hans Bergese.

In the atmosphere of those times it was not possible to produce further books though we had planned, among others, one of exercises for wind instruments.

Typenzeichnung: Dorothee Günther

Von links: 1. Spieler: Glockenspiel / 2. Spieler: Xylophon / 3. Spieler: Schellentrommel / 4. Spieler: 2 Holzblocktrommeln mit Schlägel-Gabelgriff, Rassel / 5. Spieler: Triangel, hängendes Becken, kleines Gong / 6. Spieler: 1 Pauke / 7. Spieler: 2 Pauken

In the preface to the first Schulwerk book containing pieces for performance (E 2) Keetman writes:

"In these pieces the individual players are given the task of playing several instruments of different kinds at the same time. This will improve their playing technique and extend the diversity of tone colour in ensemble playing.

The pieces should be played as chamber music. The percussion should be played appropriately and sensitively. It is impossible to do more than indicate the many nuances that lie within the nature of these instruments. Only a lively, tonally imaginative interpretation can do these pieces justice. Aim at a performance from memory from the start in order to become deeply immersed in the tone qualities of the pieces.

Should these pieces be used as an accompaniment to movement or dance it will then in any case be necessary to memorise them."

Typenzeichnung: Dorothee Günther

Von links: 1. Spieler: Glockenspiel / 2. Spieler: Xylophon, chinesische Trommel / 3. Spieler: Große Rahmentrommel, 2 Holzblocktrommeln, 2 chinesische Trommeln, Schellentrommel, Gong / 4. Spieler: Castagnette, Handtrommel, Rassel / 5. Spieler: 4 Pauken. Am linken Ständer: Chinesisches Schlitztrömmelchen, Becken, Triangel. Am rechten Ständer: Triangel, Großes Gong, Kleines Gong.

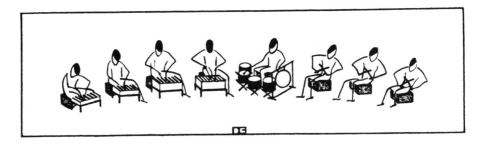

134

FURTHER EXTENSION OF THE INSTRUMENTARIUM

At my suggestion Maendler built metallophones in 1932, at first soprano and alto, then also bass. This time his own instruments could act as models rather than the Javanese instruments in their various forms. The new instruments had a magical, binding sound and gave depth and a pedal note effect to the ensemble. At the same time Maendler completed the xylophone range by adding a bass of particular resonance. It was a masterpiece that greatly enriched the lower registers of the ensemble.

A list of all the instruments used at that time in the dance orchestra and also in teaching may give an overall picture of the diversity of possible orchestrations:

Soprano and alto glockenspiels
Chromatic glockenspiels
Soprano, alto and bass xylophones
Soprano, alto and bass metallophone

Sopranino, soprano, alto, tenor and bass recorders

Musical glasses
Triangle
Small cymbals
Antique cymbals
Dance cymbals
Large cymbals
Small and large gongs
Small and large tam-tams
Bells

Castanets
Wood blocks
Cylindrical wood blocks
Wooden bells
Slit drums

Rattles and strung rattles
Jingles and strung jingles
Claves (wood or bamboo)

Tambours in various sizes
Tambourines
Chinese tom-tom
Double-skinned drum

Dance timpani
Timpani
Tenor drums
Side drum
Bass drum

Portative*
Spinet*
Fidels*
Viols*
Double bass

It was not possible to use all these instruments when the new Schulwerk edition "Musik für Kinder" (Music for Children) appeared in 1948. They had mostly been lost when the Güntherschule was bombed and they had to be remade over the years by Klaus Becker of Studio 49. Metallophones and bass xylophones were therefore not allowed for in the first volumes of "Musik für Kinder". Today these instruments can of course be used with the first exercises (see "Paralipomena")

*first used in the dance orchestra after 1934

Bass metallophone, alto metallophone, alto glockenspiel, soprano glockenspiel

Bass xylophone and recorders (bass, tenor, alto, soprano, sopranino)

Glasses, Cymbals (bottom and top left: Turkish; top right: Chinese),
bells and antique cymbals (crotales)

Wood blocks, slit drums

Tambours, double-skinned drum, tom-tom, tambourine, claves, wooden bell

Timpani, dance timpani

Bass drum, tenor drums, side drum

Gong, five different tam-tams

Timpani practice

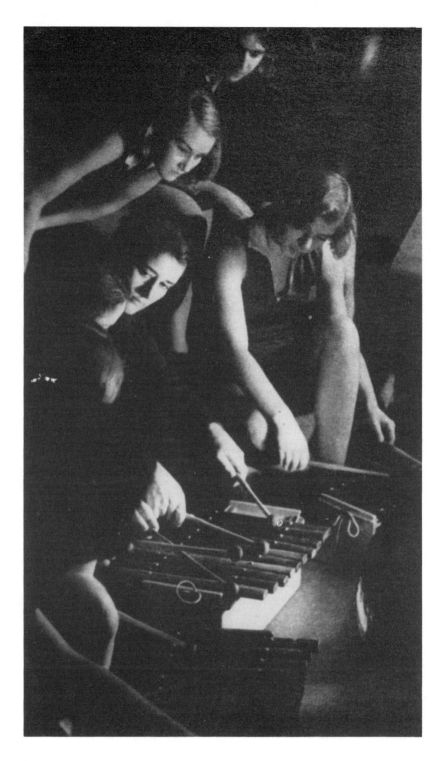

Xylophone teaching

146

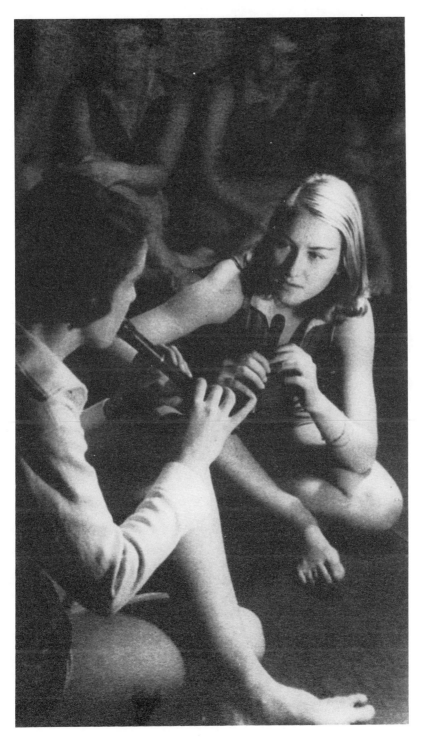

Recorder lessons

Combined percussion

Small ensemble

148

Improvisation with large ensemble

DANCE GROUP AND DANCE ORCHESTRA

"Out of movement, music,
Out of music, movement."

Dorothee Günther

Keetman had for some time been the leading personality concerned with the building up of our orchestra. She composed a series of practice exercises and pieces for recorders, xylophones and other percussion instruments, and wrote as an examination task a recorder primer from which most of the pieces were later published as part of the Orff-Schulwerk series.

Over the years a dance group with its own orchestra was formed out of the close collaboration of Lex and Keetman. A far cry from "New German Dance" with Wigman's imprint, and from "German expressive dance", it sought its own, elemental style. The foundation consisted of rhythm in its unlimited variability and the differentiated dynamic structures that arose from it, that in turn affected the use of space and thus created form.

The dance group arose from the circle of female students of the Güntherschule. The special nature of the training enabled the most gifted of them to take part both as dancers and as musicians in the group that numbered 14 - 16. Only in this way was it possible for dancers and musicians — a unity, so to speak — often to exchange roles in every performance. A unique contact between dancers and players developed, for the dancers that were playing the music, being particularly sensitive, could react to every nuance of tempo or dynamics.

Group dances with their own rules of form and their inherent dynamics usually came *before* the music, according to the ideas of the choreographer; the music grew stepwise as the dance composition unfolded, forming a unity together. The sustaining melody and the characteristic accompanying parts, as well as purely rhythmic dance accompaniments with all possible gradations of colour, formed the foundation in sound for the dance. To this individual members of the group often contributed ideas that were tried out and evaluated by everyone together. There arose a music, that, born of the same impulse, had the power to intensify and direct the dance.

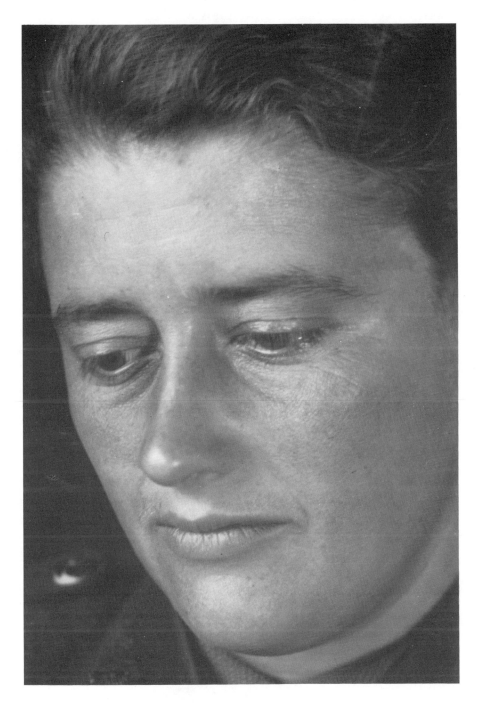

Gunild Keetman, 1930

For solo dances Lex also had an idea of the content and approximately how it would take shape. After some thorough discussion Keetman made a first musical sketch that was used as a basis for the dance, and that could later be expanded and adapted to the details of the dance that were by then fixed. Solo dances could be accompanied with a richer variety of tone, whereas in the group dances there were fewer players available, each having to play more than one instrument either simultaneously or one after the other, thereby developing a special and in some cases virtuoso technique.

The individual parts that were decided upon during rehearsals were notated in sketch form by the players as an aid to memory and later, once the whole had been finally decided, put together in a score.

Instruments such as recorders, small and large cymbals, tambours and tambourines, claves, castanets, jingles and rattles were often played by the dancers themselves while they danced.

The work in the dance group would not have been possible without the very unusual commitment of all who participated and that they took for granted. There were weeks when about 20 and more rehearsal hours were added to the usual 30 periods that most students had. Nevertheless the feeling of inner enrichment always compensated for the tension that sometimes led to psychological and physical exhaustion.

THREE DANCES
Auftakt, Bolero, Nachtlied

Auftakt (Up beat, Anacrusis)

Gunild Keetman
1930

153

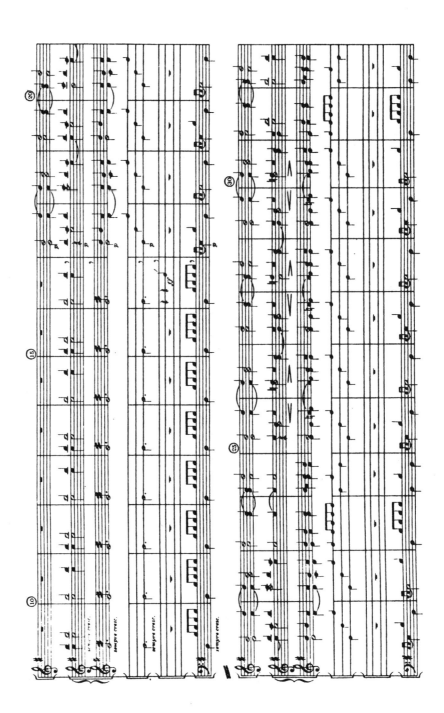

154

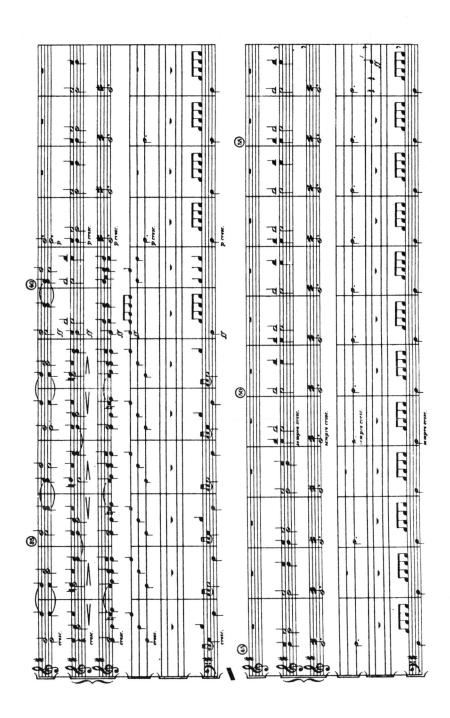

155

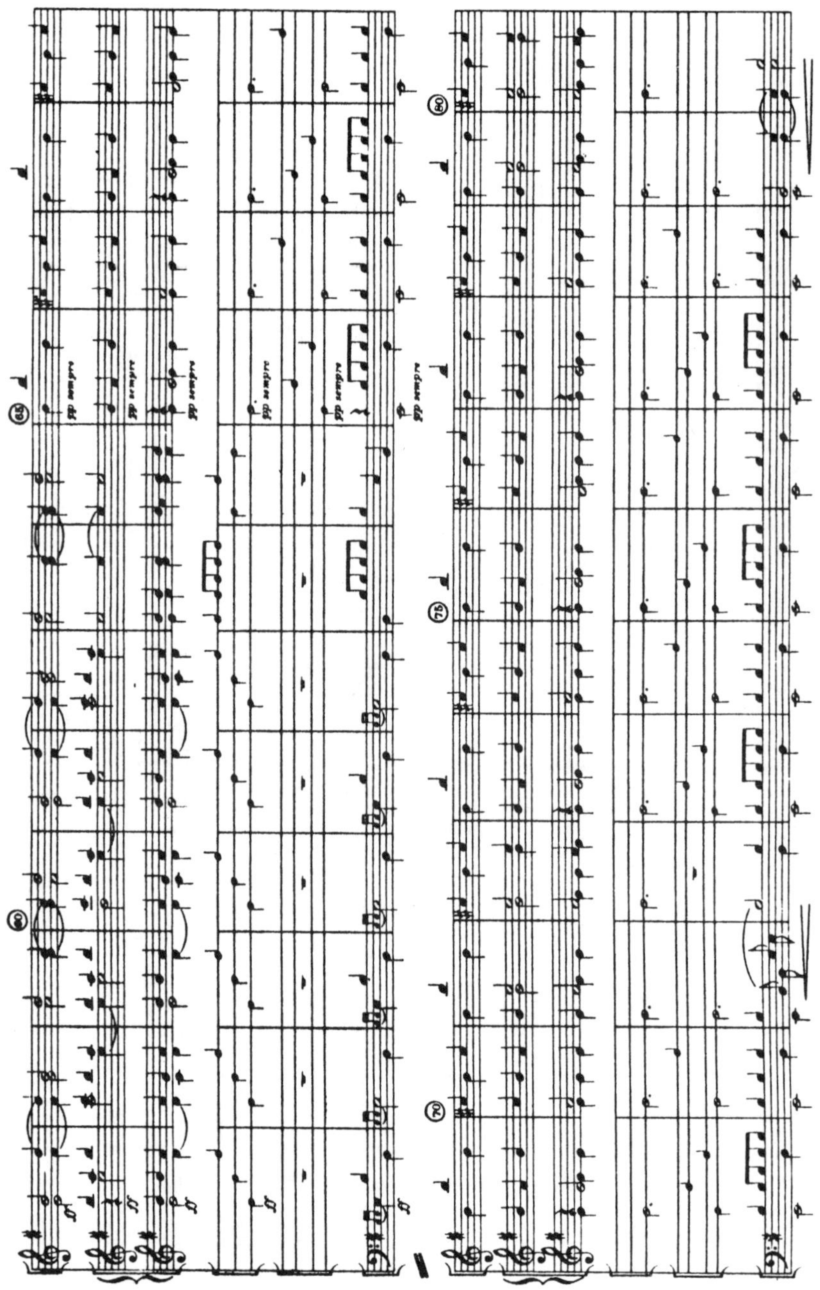

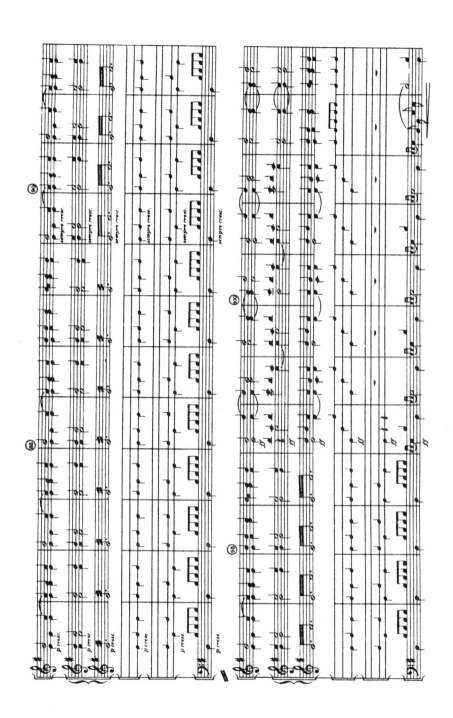

157

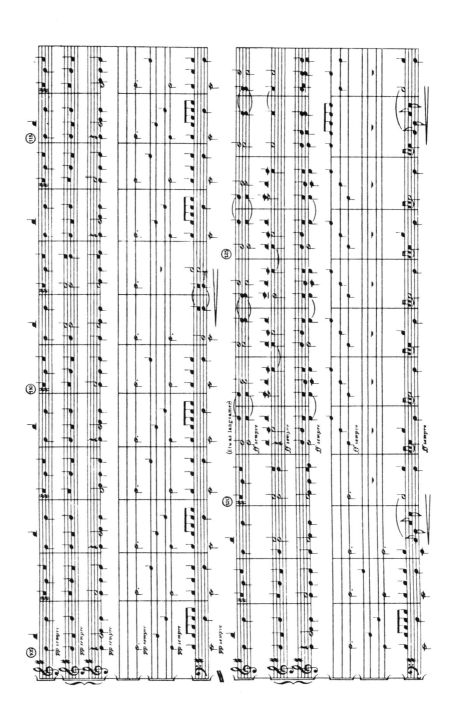

158

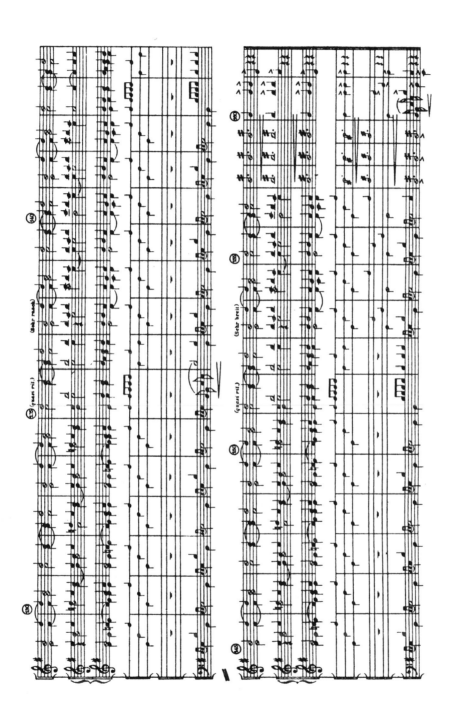

159

Bolero

Gunild Keetman
1930

160

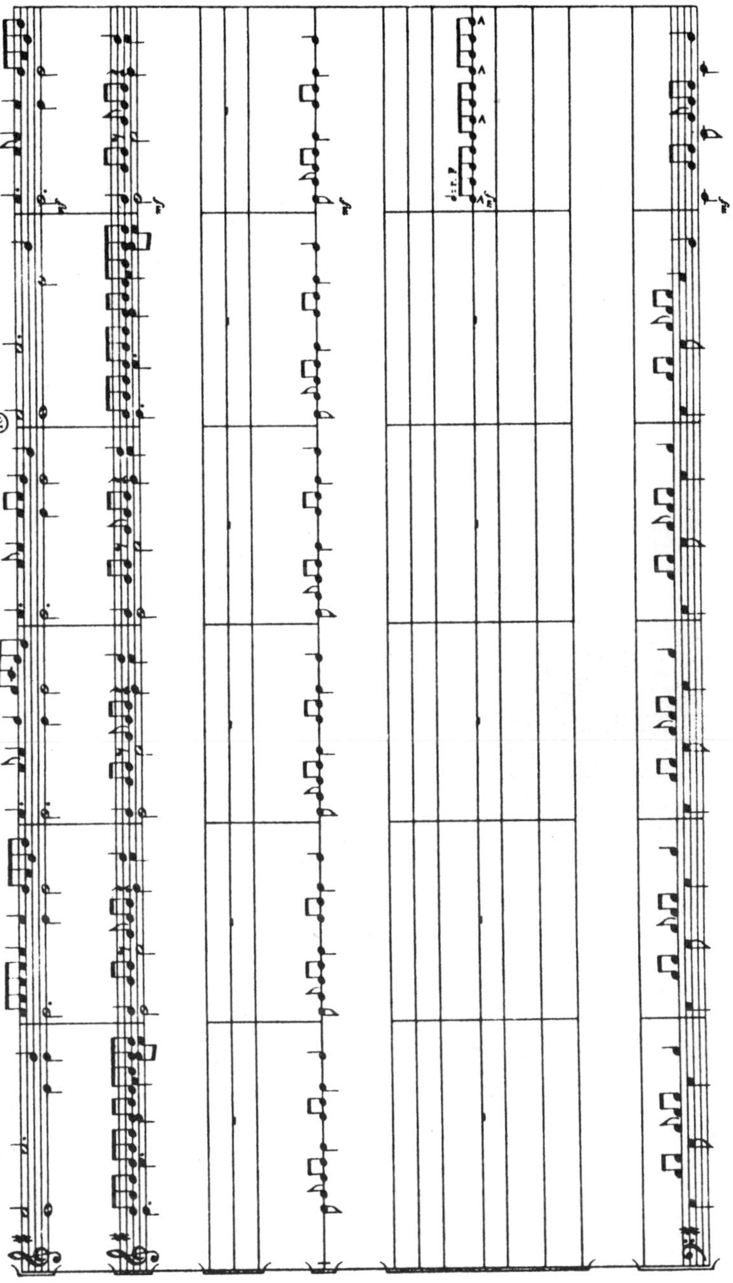

162

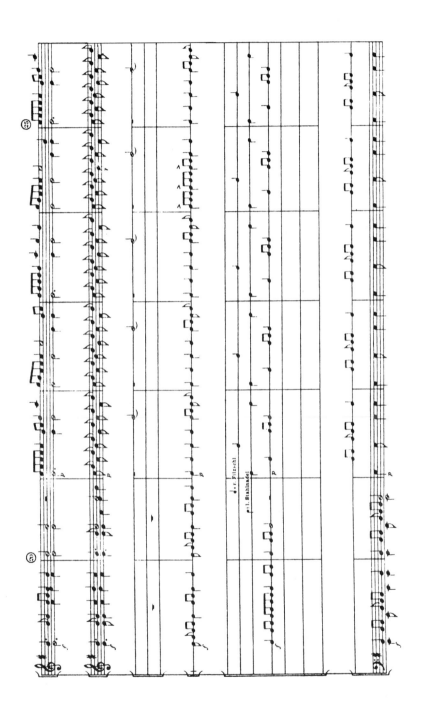

163

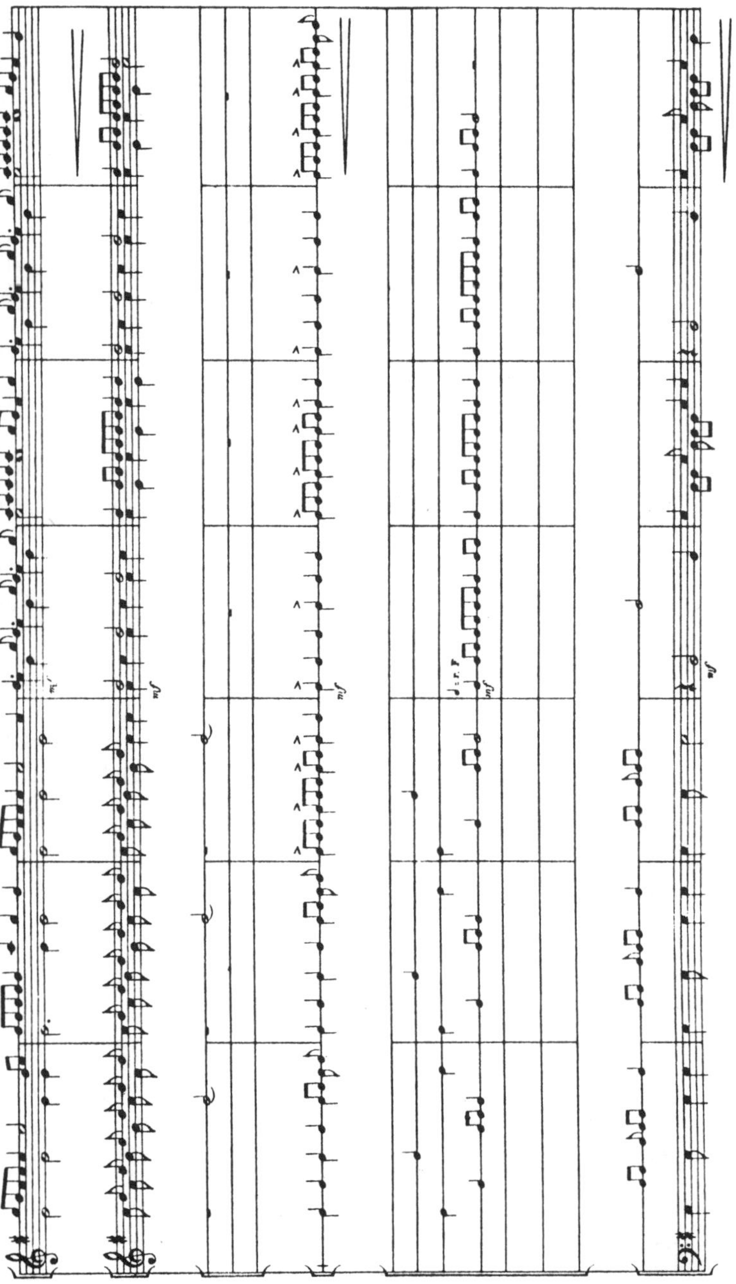
30
quasi rit.

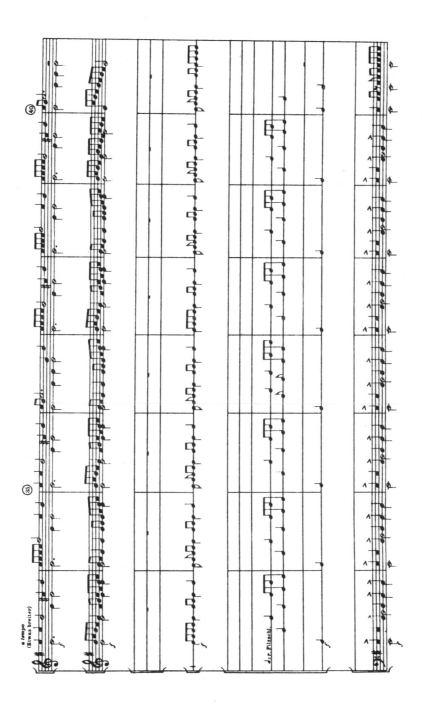

165

166

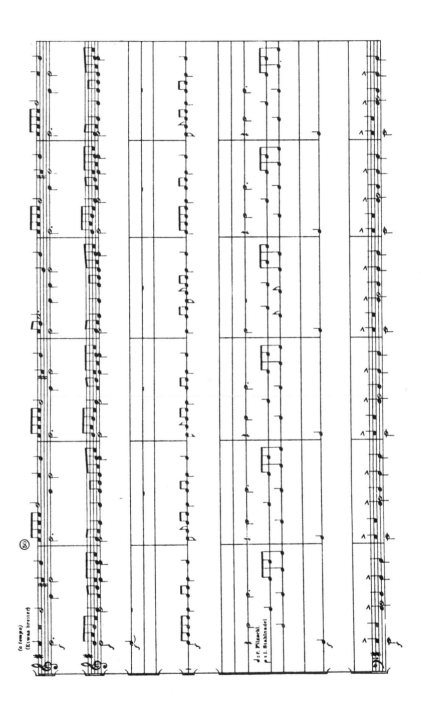

167

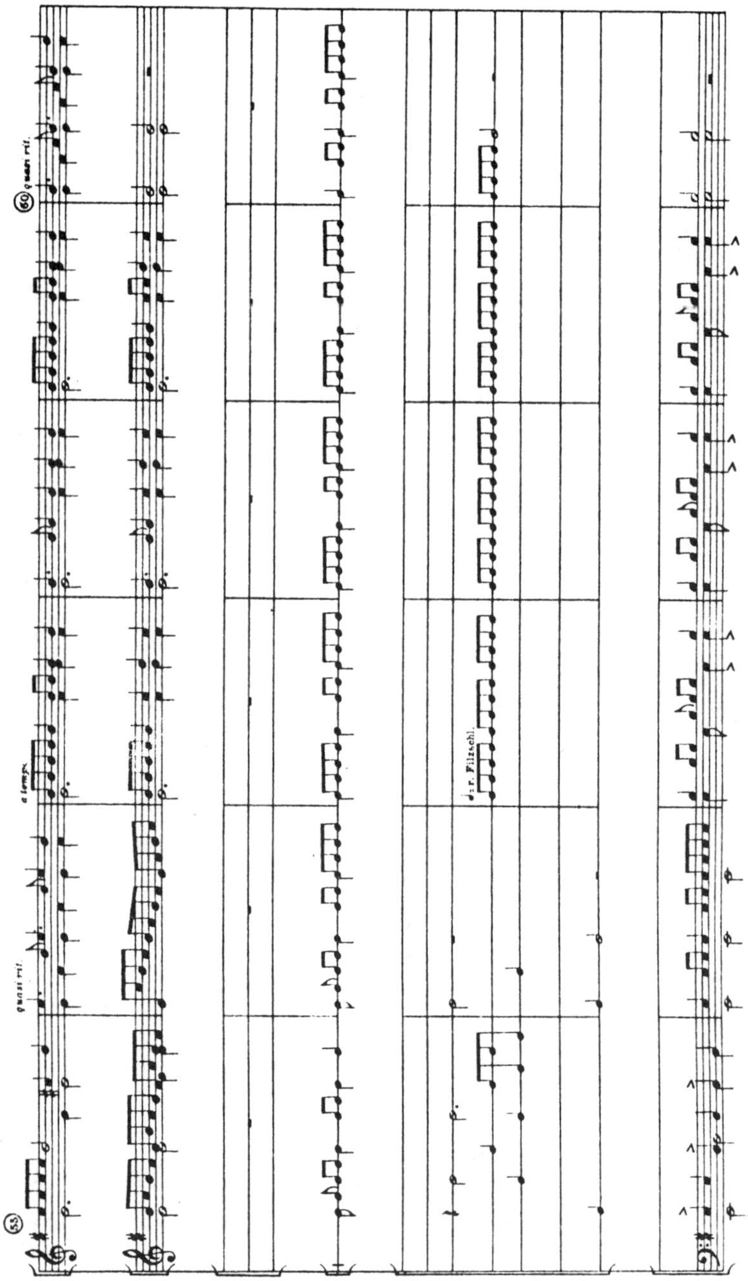
quasi rit.
a tempo
quasi rit.

169

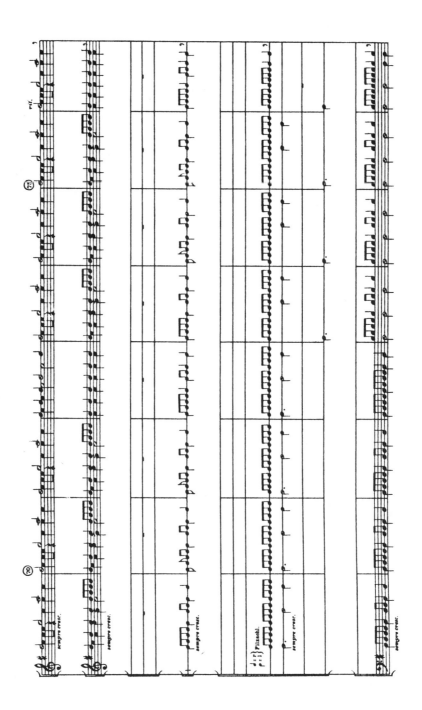

170

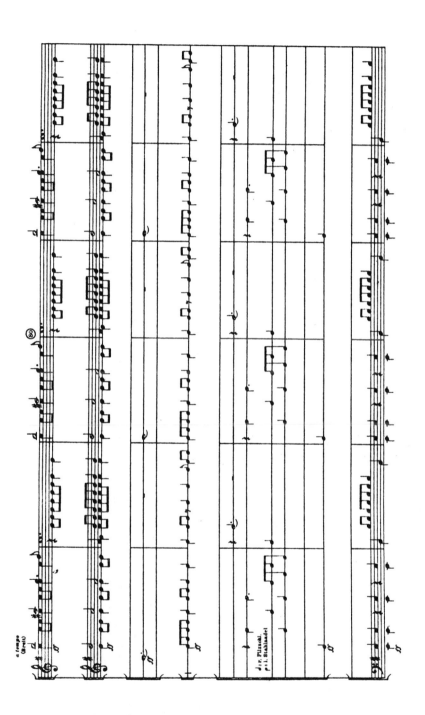

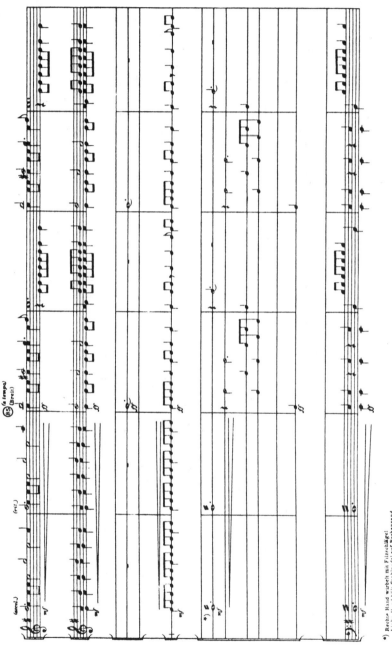

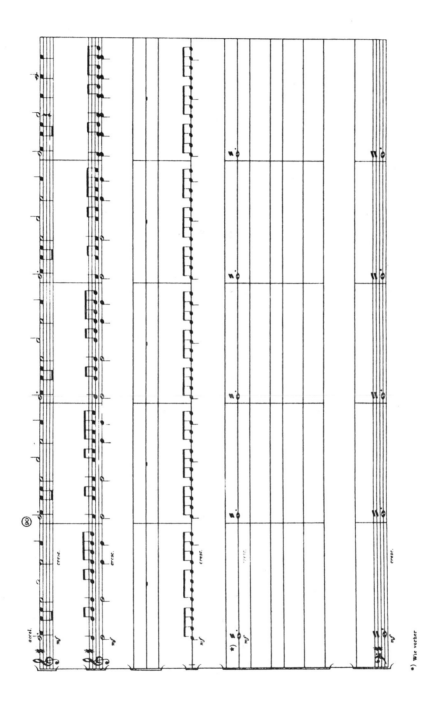

*) Wie vorher

173

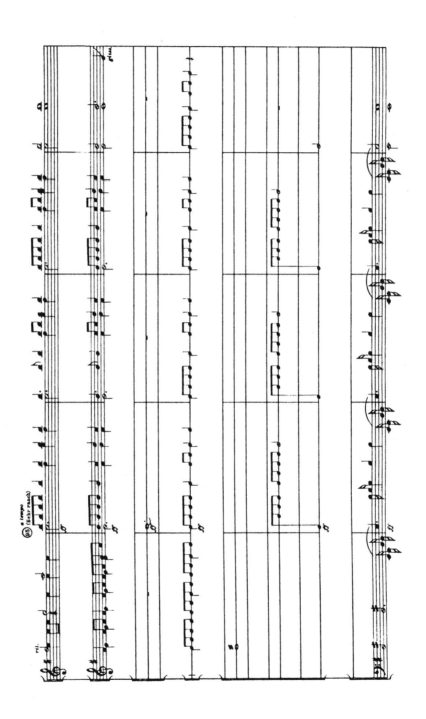

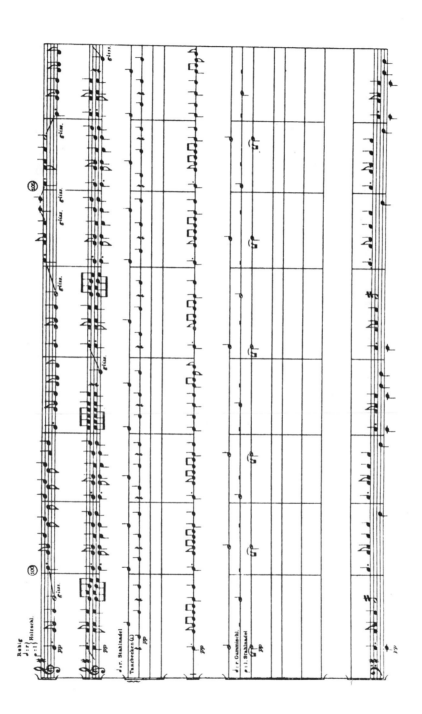

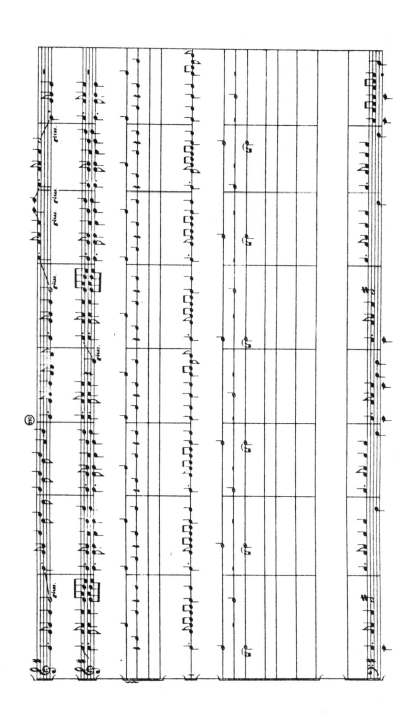

176

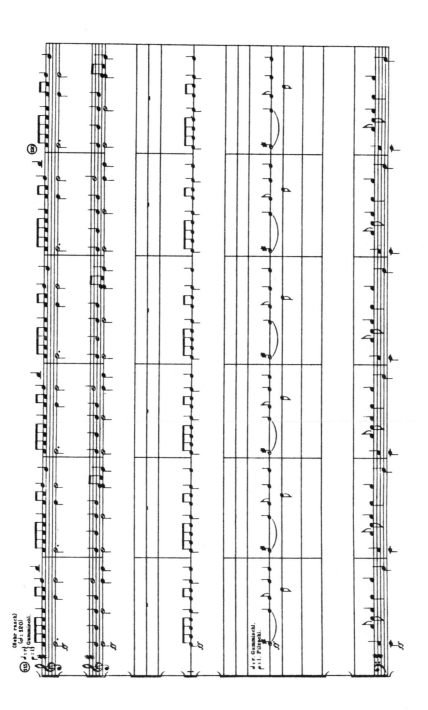

177

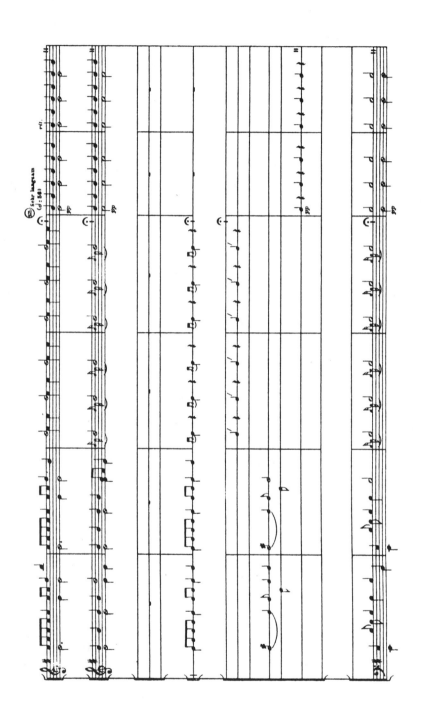

178

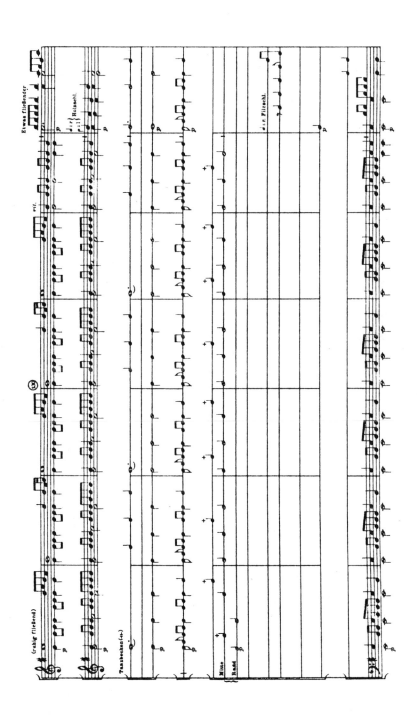

179

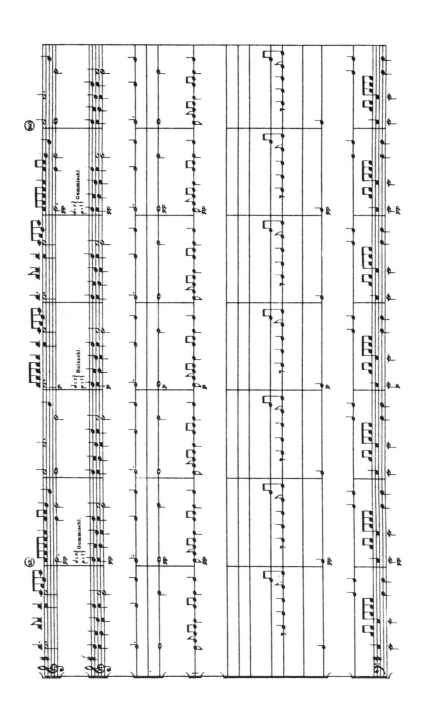

180

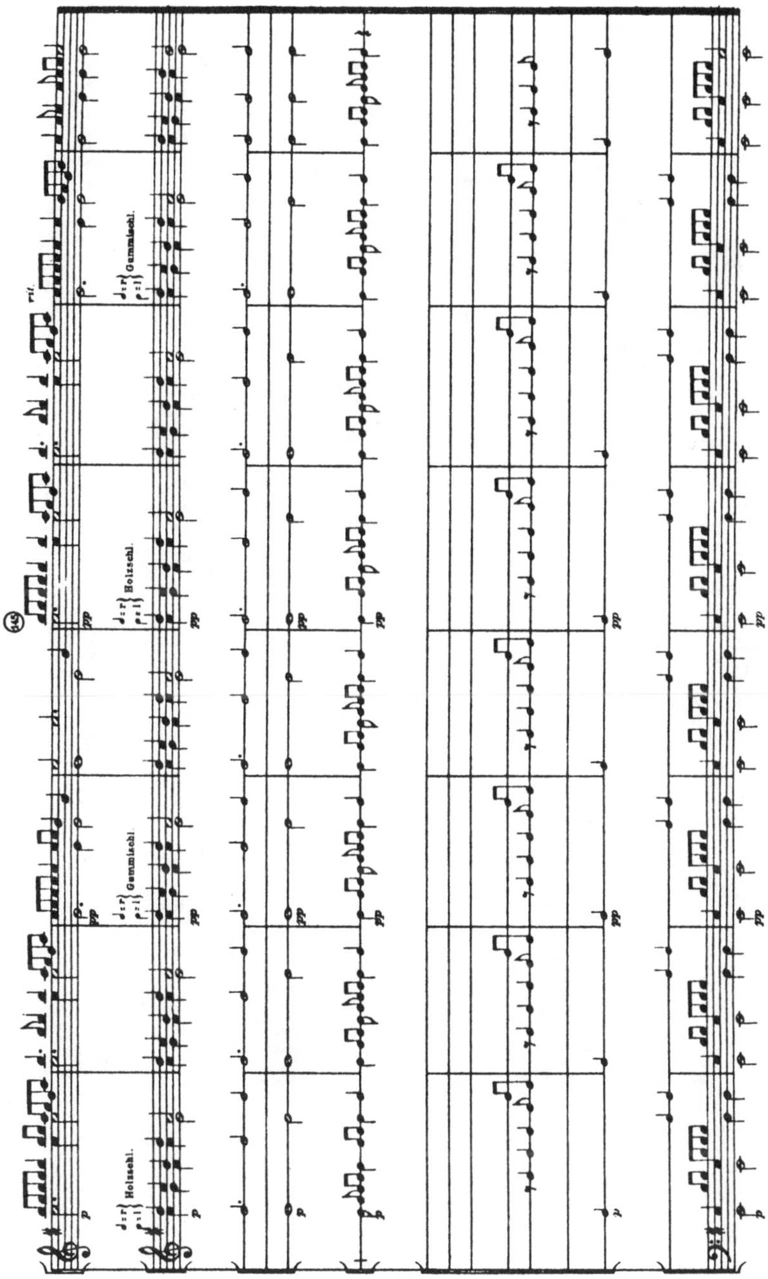
Holzschl.
Gummischl.
Holzschl.
Gummischl.
rit.

Nachtlied (Night song)

Gunild Keetman
1932

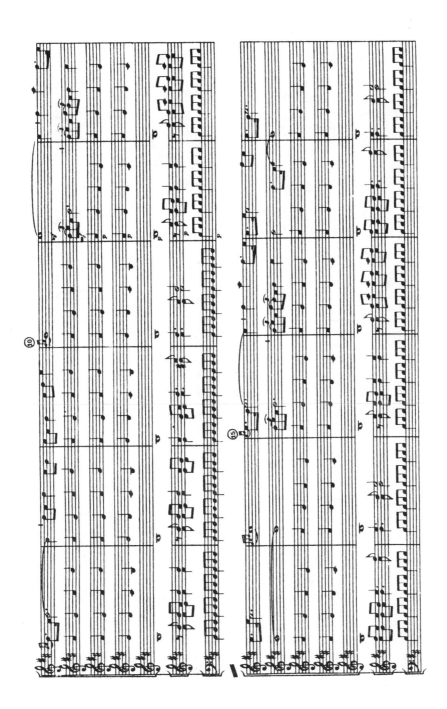

183

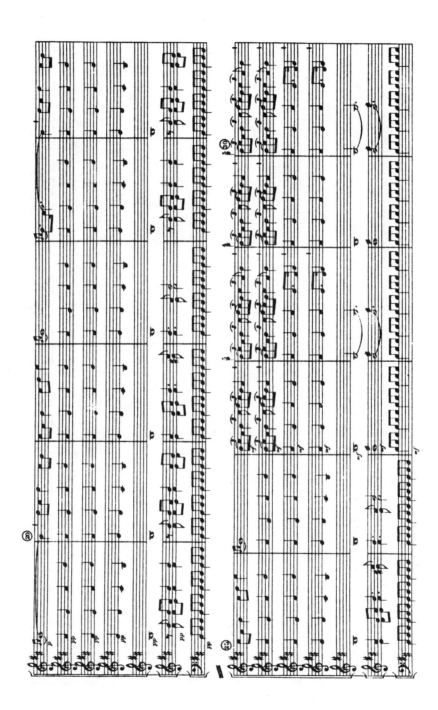

184

185

Bolero

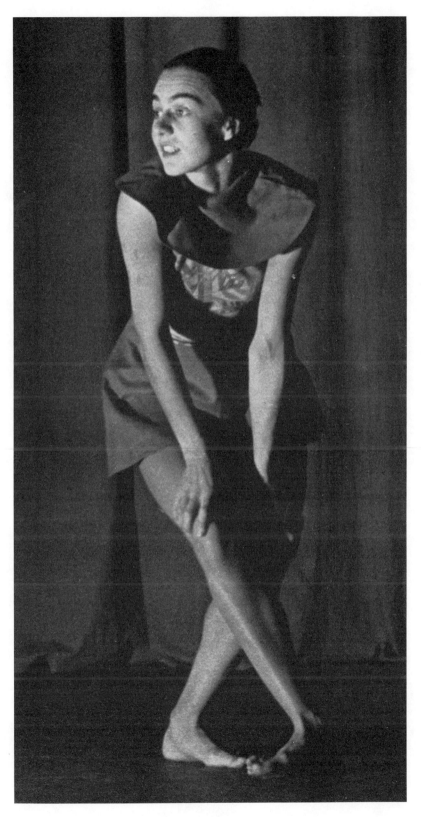

Auftakt — Up beat, anacrusis

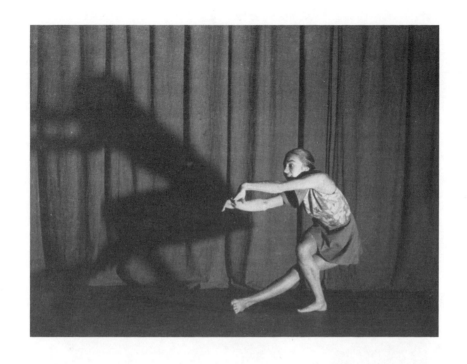

Stäbetanz — Dance of the xylophone bars

Paukentanz — Timpani dance

Paukentanz — Timpani dance

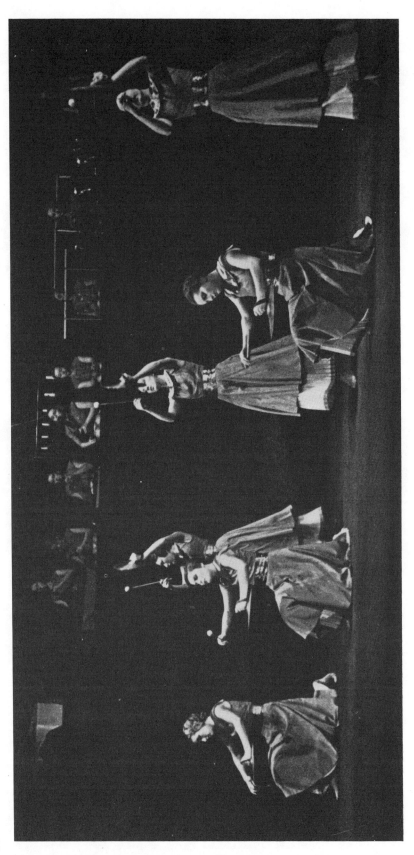

Dance with cymbals

192

Dance with cymbals

193

The dark ones

194

Jumping dance

195

The night of hovering thoughts

Maja Lex

Extracts from press comments on performances by the Günther Dance Group 1930-1934

"Der Tanz", Berlin 8. 8. 1930

Magnificent, how here, based on the New Dance, everything decadent is avoided, how a rhythmic and technical precision is achieved with organic resources. One can compare them with the precision of a ballet company — the first time in the history of the New Dance. . . . .

"New York Herald", 20.7.1930

Gunild Keetman's attractive music — here is an actual example that shows that percussion music can mean something other than deafening noise. . . . .

"Dresdner Anzeiger", 1. 7. 1930

. . . perhaps the strongest of all: a percussion orchestra of most refined cluture.

"Neue Freie Presse", Vienna, 6. 6. 1931

. . . They can book the greatest success for themselves. They are building a new dance style whose characteristic is a thrilling rhythmic intensity.

"La Revue de France", Paris, 1. 10. 1932

Few dances are so expressive as those of Maja Lex . . . One can say that the Güntherschule has created a style, and of what other school could one say that?

"Paris-Midi", 19.10.32

Music and gesture are indissolubely bound together . . . Gunild Keetman deserves a special mention for her inventive originality.

"Kölnische Zeitung*, 19. 12. 1934

. . . a unity between rhythm and movement, between music and bodily expression — the ideal of a principle of dance. The players can interchange within the individual instrumental groups, and with the dancers. Everyone can do everything.

"Westfälische Landeszeitung", Dortmund, 21,12.1934

Here for the first time the relationship to music was decisively touched. The Günther group present once more the unity of music and dance as it existed in primitive and in antique cultures.

"Hamburg Fremdenblatt", 18.12.1934

. . . Thanks to the excellent pedagogic principle of a simultaneous music and dance education, the full harmony of music and dance is achieved in an almost ideal way.

MUSIC EDUCATION COURSES

I was often invited to teach Schulwerk courses, particularly after the first Schulwerk books had been published. The professional educationists had begun to notice my work. So I held the following courses:

1931 in the Musikheim at Frankfurt an der Oder;
1931 and 1932 at the town's Musikseminar in Frankfurt an der Oder
1932 at the Hochschule für Musik in Stuttgart at a study-week to celebrate their 75th anniversary;
1932 in Berlin at the Hochschule for Gymnastics, at the Seminar for folk and youth music, and at the Central Institute for Education and Training.
1933 in Bern at the Music Conservatoire.

The event at the Stuttgart study-week was my meeting with Eberhard Preussner, then Director of the Music Department of the Central Institute for Education and Training in Berlin. We knew one another by name only. Our immediate understanding and accord grew to a lifelong friendship that always had a decisive effect upon the further development of my work. Preussner first learnt about my work at the Stuttgart course and the planned "Dialogue" with following "Discussion" became a thrilling plea by Preussner for Schulwerk, sketching pictures and visions that I had not yet even thought about. He gave excellent reports of my work at the conference and prepared the way for me to his chief in Berlin, the musically powerful Leo Kestenberg. No one can better describe this unique man than Preussner did on the occasion of his 70th birthday:

"To write about Leo Kestenberg is to write about Berlin in the 'twenties. For he was one of the strongest and most successful exponents of this unique time in a unique city. It was by no means so much the often-vaunted or defamed, slick tempo of this intensely living city that for a decade put a stamp on it as on no other city, but rather the auspicious working together of many different forces,

M O N T A G 20. Juni, 20 Uhr	Eröffnungsmusik: Paul Gross „Spielmusik" für Streicher, Trompeten und Flöten (Urauff.) Hochschulorchester. Leitung Carl Wendling. Begrüssungen. Vortrag: Dr. Paul Friedrich Scherber: Hochschule und Laienmusik. Kantate: Hermann Reutter „Der glückliche Bauer" (Urauff.) Hochschulchor u. -orchester. Leitung Hugo Holle.
D I E N S T A G 21. Juni, Vormittag 10 Uhr	Klingende Ausstellung: Neue Spielmusik für Streicher (Bartok, Hindemith, Kadosa, Seiber) Ausführende: Streichorchester der Frauenortsgruppe des Reichsverbands D.T. u. M. Leitung Catharina Bosch-Möckel. Neue Spielmusik für Klavier (Bartok, Casella, Hindemith, Reutter, Toch) Ausführende: Studierende der Hochschule für Musik.
Nachmittag 15 Uhr	Praktische Arbeit mit den Teilnehmern: Dirigierübung, Improvi- sation, Schlagzeugorchester. Leitung Carl Orff.
Abend 20 Uhr	Vortrag: Carl Orff „Elementare Musikübung, Improvisation u. Laienschulung" (mit Lichtbildern und Demonstrationen).
M I T T W O C H 22. Juni, Vormittag 8 Uhr	Praktische Arbeit mit den Teilnehmern: Dirigierübung; Improvi- sation mit Instrumenten (Schlagzeug, Klavier, Xylophon) Leitung Carl Orff.
Nachmittag 15 Uhr	Musizierstunde der höheren Schule. Leitung Karl Aichele. Vortrag: Karl Aichele „Neues Musizieren in der Schule". Musizierstunde der Volksschule: Singen und Musizieren mit Melodie- u. Schlaginstrumenten Leitung Gust. Wirsching. Übungsschule des Musiklehrerseminars der Hochschule für Musik: Hans Brehme „Kleine Kantate" für Kinder- chor, Blockflöten, Violinen, 2 Klaviere und Schlag- zeug (Urauff.) Leitung P. Fr. Scherber.
Abend 20 Uhr	Vortrag: Dr. Eberhard Preussner „Die Stellung des Laien in der Musik". Neue Laienmusik für Chor und Instrumente (Hindemith, L. v. Knorr, Marx u. a.) Ausführende: Der Stuttgarter Singkreis. Leitung G. Wirsching, E. Rilling.

Programme of the Music Education Study-week, Stuttgart, June 20-26, 1932

200

DONNERSTAG **FREITAG** **SAMSTAG** Vormittag 8 Uhr	Praktische Arbeit mit den Teilnehmern. Dirigierübung, Improvisation, Schlagzeugtechnik, Summ-, Klatsch- und Stampfchor, Dirigierimprovisation mit grossem Orchester. Leitung Carl Orff.
Nachmittag 14.³⁰ Uhr	Klingende Ausstellungen: Neue Sing- und Spielmusik (Butting, Finke, Jarnach, Petyrek, Seiber, Strawinsky u. a.) Ausführende: Studierende der Hochschule für Musik.
15.³⁰ Uhr	Praktische Arbeit. Carl Orff: Schulwerkübung — Chor mit Instrumenten, Blockflötenübung, Gemeinschaftsmusik.
	Ausserdem folgende Sonderveranstaltungen:
Freitag u. Samstag Nachmittag	Sondergruppen für Lehrer der Volks- und höheren Schulen. Pädagogische Aussprachen.
FREITAG 24. Juni, Abend 20 Uhr	Carl Orff: Versuchsstunde: Chorimprovisationen. Helmut Bornefeld: Lehrstück „Der weisse Storch" für Kinder, Chor, Sprecher und Publikum mit Instrumenten (Urauff.) Ausführende: Der Esslinger Kammerchor. Leitung Helmut Bornefeld.
SAMSTAG 25. Juni, 10.³⁰ Uhr	Zwiegespräch Eberhard Preussner - Carl Orff mit anschliessender Diskussion.
Abend 20 Uhr	Öffentlicher Versuchsabend: Carl Orff „Kantaten" nach Texten von Werfel. Querschnitt durch die Arbeit der Woche. Stücke aus dem „Schulwerk". Leitung: Carl Orff. Ausführende: Die Teilnehmer der Woche und Publikum.
SONNTAG 26. Juni, Vormittag	Matinée der Münchner Kammertanzbühne.

AUSSTELLUNGEN

Selbstverfertigte Schulinstrumente - Historische Instrumente für Haus- und Laienmusik - Noten und Bücher.

Sämtliche Veranstaltungen in den Räumen der Hochschule für Musik

that had something to offer that could be described as an attempt to build a new society . . .

"A city whose intellectual life was shaped by Einstein, Planck, Spengler and Spranger among many others, and where Schönberg, Schreker, Hindemith, still even Busoni, Klemperer, Furtwängler and Kleiber counted among the first in music, was indeed a metropolis of minds and music. Certainly those ten or twelve years were full of tensions that were not, however, pushed to one side, but were experienced, suffered and used. One was full of hope and of apprehension . . .

"Berlin was an example for everything and everyone, the critical conscience of Germany and perhaps also of a better Europe.

"In 1919 fate had decreed that Leo Kestenberg, in the middle of this restless, still bleeding Berlin, should introduce and develop a reformation of musical life, which, in the then closed atmosphere, would not have been possible anywhere else. Kestenberg was originally a pianist, a friend of the unique Busoni. What struck one at once was his lack of prejudice, the breadth of his vision, and his enthusiasm that carried you along with him.

"Through his Socialist Party he had an influential position in the Ministry of Culture. The way he administered his office was not for the good of the party, but for the general good. Even his political opponents had then to recognise, and must do so even more today, that Kestenberg conceived his post as a real mission. He instigated a reform of music education that outlasted the times and the political parties. Neither before nor since has there been a minister in charge of music that had such significance. . . ." (From: Eberhard Preussner, Leo Kestenberg zum 70. Geburtstag, in: Musik im Unterricht, XLIII, 1952.)

Since Preussner had given a detailed report of my work he persuaded Kestenberg to invite me to Berlin for a discussion (end of 1932). Once more a decisive meeting for me.

The rapport with Kestenberg was immediate. This was the man I needed, sovereign and provided with the full power of authority. After some further discussions he made the unexpected suggestion that Schulwerk be introduced into the Berlin schools. Before I could come to my senses he was making further arrangements: I should give special courses in Berlin for a number of specially selected music teachers, and introduce the Schulwerk way of working to them, and take further care of the experiment.

Even Preussner was surprised at the generosity of Kestenberg's spontaneous plans. For the first time I had the chance to try out my ideas on a big scale. I was quite disturbed at the abundance of possibilities that disclosed themselves.

The events that lay ahead turned out differently, however. Some weeks after our discussions Kestenberg was relieved of all his posts by the new rulers and had to leave Germany; the destruction of his life's work and the burial of my greatest hopes.

Preussner stayed in Berlin until he was appointed deputy director of the Mozarteum in Salzburg in 1939. We met there again later and renewed our collaboration.

Since our plans in Berlin were known and so closely connected with Kestenberg, my educational activity was from now on suspect in certain circles. Courses were no longer held under the title "Orff-Schulwerk", but were described as "Music and Movement" courses.

A severe depression over the way things were moving and an apprehension about what would sooner or later come to pass caused me to work less and less in public. I gave up directing the Bachverein (Bach Society) (Carl Orff and sein Wek II, p. 191/92) with whom I had realised my scenically presented concerts. My work at the radio was reduced to a minumum. My Brecht and Werfel Cantatas had to be withdrawn from the publisher's lists on account of the two authors, and we were likewise not allowed to print further Schulwerk volumes.

In 1933 Berthe Trümpy's Dance School, that came from the Wigman circle, joined the Güntherschule and became known as "Güntherschule Berlin". The Munich school remained under the direction of Dorothee Günther, the Berlin one was directed by Berthe Trümpy. There was a free exchange of tutors between the two schools.

OLYMPIC FESTIVAL

In 1934 a letter from Dr. Carl Diem, General Secretary and Organiser of the 1936 Olympic Games in Berlin, stirred me out of my lethargic reaction to all public appearances.

At the suggestion of Baron Pierre de Coubertin, the reviver of the Olympic Games, Carl Diem had written a Festival of "Olympic Youth" that was to be performed in the stadium at the opening of the games. He asked me to compose part of the music. The Festival began with "Einzug und Reigen der Kinder und Mädchen" (Children's procession and round dance) and then went on to "Dances and Games of Youth"; big solo dance scenes by Palucca, Kreutzberg (Waffentanz — War dance) and Wigman (Totenklage — Dirge) to the last movement of Beethoven's Ninth Symphony ending with the choir singing the "Ode to Joy". ·

Glass bell and musical glasses introduce the Festival

The youth orchestra of the Güntherschule conducted by Gunild Keetman

Diem felt that the style of movement and music at the Güntherschule, known to him through performances, would be specially appropriate for the opening of his Festival.

I could not give a spontaneous answer to his request. I was afraid that such an attention-attracting occasion would be connected with an encounter with certain official Berlin circles that seemed to me inopportune. Only when Diem assured me that the Festival was an international Olympic occasion that allowed no kind of political bias, did I agree to his request and only then if the contract came directly from the Olympic Committee. At the same time Günther would be responsible for the choreography and Lex would compose the dances. I hoped through this opportunity to introduce our Schulwerk work to an international forum. I was also attracted to the idea of writing music for such a spatial setting. I had already come to grips with the new technical equipment of radio and loudspeakers at an open air performance of my "Entrata" in Königsberg (Carl Orff und sein Werk, Bd. II, p. 195).

205

At first phonograph records of my music were made so that the Berlin school children and young people (approximately 6000) could learn the dances.

Children's round dance

I had given Keetman, who had been involved in the creation of the music, the responsibility of co-ordinating and directing the rehearsals and performance in the Stadium. She conducted our dance orchestra, enlarged to 30 players who, thanks to its special composition and to the expert technical facilities, were able to fill the huge stadium with their sound. A minor sensation was caused by the very first sound, one glass bell, struck close to the microphone, that spread an enchantingly magical sound over the entire stadium. The remaining instrumentation was delicate and transparent: glasses, recorders, viols, guitars; fundamental string bass and a melody-carrying oboe were supported by a choir of barred instruments — xylophones, metallophones and glockenspiels. Timpani, cymbals and small percussion gave the rhythmic accentuation. The press both at home and abroad wrote extremely positively about Günther's production, and about the music and the dance.

206

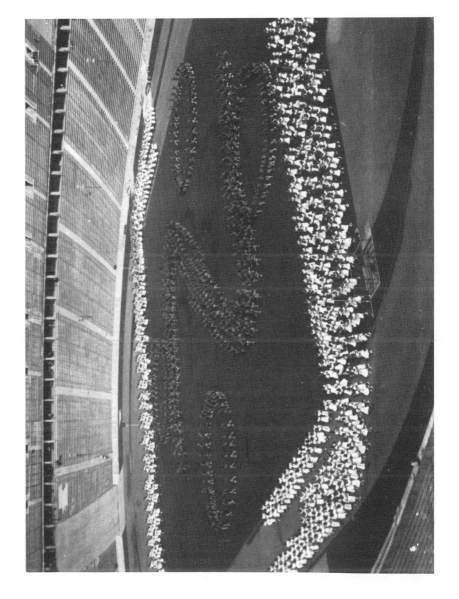

The Round Dance (rehearsal by day)

In spite of a great success the "echo" of my olympic work was disappointing. Only Japan who was due to have the Olympic Games in 1940 was receptive to my work and wanted to make a similar contract with me. Because of the war these plans came to nothing. I was sorry for I felt that especially in Japan I would find an understanding and readiness to accept my work. This conjecture proved absolutely justified when "Musik für Kinder" later reached Japan.

The handwritten original score of the music "Olympische Reigen" (Olympic round dance) is lost. "Einzug und Reigen der Kinder" (Children's procession and round dance) was published without the details of the instruments. (Schott).

"Einzug der Mädchen" (Girls' procession) was taken from a preserved sketch and included in a new version in Volume III of Music for Children where it is called "Einzug" and "Festive Procession" in the German and English editions respectively.

THE LAST YEARS OF THE GÜNTHERSCHULE

In 1936 the Güntherschule was able to move into a building that corresponded to its needs, with halls and many lesser rooms, at No. 16 Kaulbachstrasse near the English Garden. This brought to an end the permanently cramped conditions and the need to make use of halls outside the school.

The Güntherschule in the Kaulbachstrasse in Munich

But the "late hours" for new experiments were no longer available. Since 1933 I had very much reduced my activity at the school so that by 1936 I was only available for the examinations. I was dedicating myself almost exclusively to composition with which my subconscious mind had long been active and was now exerting pressure from inside.

The dance group unflinchingly continued to give their performances up to the war years, often under the most difficult conditions and often very much reduced in numbers.

The Güntherschule in Berlin-Wilmersdorf (formerly Trümpy-Schule)

In the end the ever-increasing transport problems made it impossible to transport large percussion cases. Pianos had often to be substituted, which brought the whole idea and purpose of the work into question. On top of this came the ever-increasing annoyances caused by the Party. When Günther energetically resisted some forceful political decree, the Gauleiter (area commander in the Nazi time) for the city of Munich confiscated the school building for his own use in July 1944. The school had to be closed and the teaching was discontinued. Some of the tutors were drafted to military service and the others dispersed in all directions. The whole inventory of school equipment could not be taken out in the twinkling of an eye and stored somewhere else, nor was there any pressure to do so. It was clear that the "necessary confiscation" was only a pretence to force the school to close.

When, on the 7th January, 1945, the school was bombed and burnt out the result was the loss of the entire inventory, the archives, library, store of photographs, all educational materials and equipment and most of the to some extent irreplaceable instruments and all the costumes.

That was the end of the Güntherschule, a school that is still a legend today.

SCHULWERK AT THE BAYERISCHEN RUNDFUNK

The political wave had long since swept away all the ideas developed in Schulwerk as undesirable, and the complete collapse of the year 1945 left only ruins everywhere.

Then there came to me unexpectedly, improbably, a new call.

It came in 1948, verbally, in the form of a telephone request from the Bayerischen Rundfunk (Bavarian Radio). Dr. Panofsky, a colleague at the Bavarian Radio, an ever-understanding friend who was also well-acquainted with my work, had found a copy of that record "Einzug und Reigen der Kinder und Mädchen" from the Festival of the 9th Olympic Games, Berlin, 1936, in an antique shop. He had played it to the head of the schools broadcasts, Annemarie Schambeck. She had never heard any Schulwerk music before and was so affected by it that she spontaneously asked me: "Can you write music like this that children could play themselves? We believe that this kind of music appeals especially to them, and we are thinking of a series of broadcasts."

At that time I was working on my score of Antigone and had turned away from all educational considerations. I was nevertheless attracted by the proposition, for it was not a revival of something that had come to an end but was a new beginning with new materials and a new aim. To send out a series of programmes to hundreds of schools for thousands of children was an attractive idea, an idea of such dimensions as the one I had dreamt of with Kestenberg. If I had already had many years experience with Schulwerk it had nevertheless been with young people and adults, and it had formed part of their professional training that aspired to different educational and artistic aims. What I was now being offered was something completely different. A music exclusively for children that could be played, sung and danced by them but that could also in a similar way be invented by them — a world of their own.

Wißt ihr, wie auch der Kleine nah ist? Ju mach
des Kleine

Recht, den Großer begehrt just so des Großer zu Thun.

Ludwig Richter.
auch ein Kleinmeister.

Dresden. 1884.

I was well aware that rhythmic training should start in early childhood. The unit of music and movement, that young people in Germany have to be taught so laboriously, is quite natural to a child. It was also clear to me what Schulwerk had so far lacked: apart from a start, in the Güntherschule we had not allowed the word or the singing voice its fully rightful place. The natural starting point for work with children is the children's rhyme, the whole riches of the old, appropriate children's songs. The recognition of this fact gave me the key for the new educational work.

Children (at the radio) make music . . .

... for children in the school

Already in 1930 the publisher Schott had made a pre-announcement of the coming publication "Music for Children" and said it would be complemented with "Music by Children", but next to all my usual work at that period I did not have the time to work out an elemental way of teaching music. Newly accosted, the ideas came once again to the surface and I decided to accept the offer of the Bavarian Radio.

I worked with Gunild Keetman to put together the material. We prepared the series with a group of children eight to twelve years old, and with the remains of the instruments from the Güntherschule. An experienced teacher, Rektor Rudolf Kirmeyer spoke the connecting texts and gave the information.

Walter Panofsky wrote thus about these early days:

"On September 15th 1948, the first Schulwerk programmes were broadcast over the air from Munich. No one had any idea of the kind of echo they might arouse. Even on the technical side the situation was far from good. Only a few Bavarian schools were able to listen to the Schulwerk programmes. They were sent out therefore into a wide-open, almost echoless space. Today, looking back from a distance, that first programme appears as an extraordinary feat of pioneer work, as a thrust into a new educational land.

"The programmes that came into being under Orff's direction avoided long theoretical instructions. Children made music for children and with children. The example that came over the loudspeaker had only to be copied, and then later developed further. The old children's rhyme "ich und du" (me and you) that was the centrepiece of the first programme had, unintentionally, something very symbolic about it.

"Annemarie Schambeck had accepted fourteen programmes proposed by Orff, she had decided to present them even if there was no echo, or perhaps even strong opposition from the schools. It showed how crucial it was that an independent, non-educational institution made Schulwerk its own. Had it been started by a single school it would have taken a long time to reach the outside world; through the radio it could spread over the whole region. The echo was, from the beginning, surprisingly large, and it increased with every programme."

It was soon clear that it would not rest with the planned few broadcasts, but that this was the seed of a development that could not yet be seen.

The instruments excited the performers as well as the children listening in the schools. They wanted to make music in this way too. The necessary instruments were missing and there came ever more questions as to where such instruments could be obtained.

At this time Maendler did not want to have anything more to do with the making of Schulwerk instruments. His age, the loss of his workshop and the lack of palisander wood made such a work seem impossible to him. Here Klaus Becker sprang into the breach and

Klaus Becker, 1948

built xylophones with the materials that were at hand, as well as he could. He had worked with Maendler and he had helped Maendler build xylophones for the first performance of my "Antigone". The first xylophones were made from the shelves of a built-in cupboard in a flat that had been bombed. All kinds of woods were used to make the bars, birch, pine, elm, walnut, sycamore.

Soon the radio was able to institute competitions for the school children and the prizes nearly always consisted of instruments made by Becker. The task for the children was to make up tunes and accompaniments to given rhymes and to write them down. The best were performed in the next broadcast. The gratifyingly large response, and the good results, showed that the broadcasts were being properly understood and carried out.

Under the influence of this unexpected response, Walter Panofsky wrote in the Radio magazine (April 1949), "Orff-Schulwerk, a statement of accounts":

". . . The numerous letters and essays, questions and stimuli that have been sent in during this last half year give credence to the high pedagogical value of this musical work. It lies in education for independence. If schoolchildren send in melodies they have written — from the clumsy drawing of the staff to the nine part score sent in by a nine-year-old(!) — it is not a question of unusual talent but of children who have been awakened, for whom the elemental originality of the Schulwerk way of making music has released in them musical powers, that, if their musical education remains solely reproductive, stay buried. This is by no means to say that work with Schulwerk should exclude the other . . ."

Within one year after our first broadcast, with materials easier to get and the demand growing constantly, Becker was able to found his workshop for making instruments "Studio 49" — a piece of luck for Schulwerk and my further work. As in the 'twenties the development of Schulwerk as I had imagined it would have been impossible without Maendler, so without Becker the new start after the collapse of everything, and also the spreading of the Schulwerk idea both at home and abroad would have been unthinkable.

Becker's achievement was not only in the resumption of Maendler's talented work, but, under the new conditions, a creative development. He not only thought of tonal improvements on Maendler's originals, but built a child's string instrument, the "Bordun", and new instrument types that I needed for the realisation of my ideas as a composer, such as a lithophone, wooden drums, large wood blocks and others.

Bordun

After the unexpected success of the first broadcasts Annemarie Schambeck came to me with a further request. She asked if I could write for this year a Christmas play for children. In spite of some misgivings, for the time was rather short, I accepted the commission.

Within a few days I had written the text and Keetman, apart from a few additions from me, had written all the music.

"Christmas and Nativity plays are nowhere found so frequently or so deeply rooted in the land and the people as in the mountain regions of Bavaria and Austria. They seem to have an innate, genuine passion for their theatrical heritage of the material of the story of Christ's birth, that for hundreds of years they have presented in countless ways and interspersed with native customs." (Paul Winter)

220

From earliest childhood crib scenes and nativity plays were familiar to me. I made them up for myself. I could not have imagined such a tradition-bound activity without the Bavarian landscape and dialect. Another feature was that it was a real "boyish" activity, the terms of expression corresponding to the young producer. The angel of the Annunciation was played by a boy. For this reason and through the strength of the dialect all possibility of false sentimentality was excluded.

On 24th December 1948 one such play was given its first broadcast performance. It was produced by me, sung and acted by children and accompanied by a Schulwerk type instrumental ensemble under the direction of Karl List. From then on it was repeated every year.

About this broadcast Rudolf Bach wrote:
"The style of this "Weihnachtsgeschichte" (Christmas Story) is of fundamental significance and the quality of its text and music has finally made a whole pile of sentimental nativity plays of indifferent sincerity from the days of late romantic decadence, look like waste paper.

"It is intended for performance by child speakers and singers, not only just intended but also really suitable. For it possesses what so seldom endures: the genuine innocence of perception and discovery, in which the mystery of Christ's birth appears as something that has just happened for the first time, and at the same time as long since fulfilled, deeply familiar, whereby all the varied events of that night of wonder are only evoked through the to and fro exchange of words shared by the shepherd onlookers.

"There are wonderful moments in this peasant discourse: lively and arresting, naively happy and tender, fervent, touching the heart. The music that portrays the worldly and the other worldly "out there", has a pregnant melodic quality and is subtle in its sound textures. One of the strongest scenes is the arrival of the Three Kings, where speech and music, in all simplicity, meet in the detached greatness of an almost liturgical ceremony . . . "

("Münchner Tagebuch", 21.1.49)

The play that had been written for Bavarian Radio was soon taken up and broadcast by other radio stations. Apart from this there were countless performances in churches and schools, soon also in other dialects. The transfer to more cultivated speech, (the original is in Bavarian dialect M.M.) however, would destroy the basic texture of the sound that is so necessary for this play. In Holland it is performed as "Kerstwonder" or "Kerstspel" — in English it has traversed half the world as the "Christmas Story".

Of the many different presentations I would like to mention two films that impressed me particularly. One was commissioned by the Westdeutschen Rundfunk in 1964 and was filmed in the famous medieval church of the Convent Nonnberg in Salzburg. Two groups of boys, Tobi-Reiser-Buben and Tölzer Knabenchor, under the direction of Gerhard Schmidt-Gaden, did the speaking and singing. The shepherd scenes in the fields were played in the crypt, those round the crib in a corner of the church, and the Gloria in the organ gallery. It was my wish that the part of Mary should be taken by a boy. The photograph should make the rightness of this decision understandable.

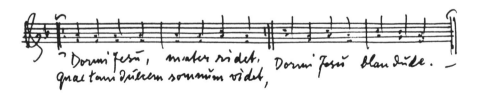

The second film was made in 1975 and comes from the work of the well-known producer and puppeteer, Peter Grassinger, who offered the Bavarian Radio a new solution that he himself described as an experiment. The black and white photographs can only give a pale impression of the liveliness of the scene in which colour and light play such an important part. Grassinger writes:

"In filming the Christmas Story we tried to combine three different styles. The shepherd boys are alive and move from their fire, traverse the wintry landscape of the Lower Alps till they come to the crib; the events at the crib are presented in alternation between puppets and figurines.

"The dramatic impulses emanate from the Three Kings who, as puppets together with Joseph and Mary, bring to life the previous scene with the figurines. The lively expressions on the carved faces are revealed by torchlight. In the conception of this film I was considerably influenced by an intensive preoccupation with the music during the early stages, for it is particularly the elemental qualities of Schulwerk that suit the movements of a puppet, so that a combination can give valuable stimulus to the puppet play and a visual enrichment to Schulwerk."

In one of the early Keetman books "Spielstücke für kleines Schlagwerk" there is a piece that is included in the recordings (Musica Poetica N. 4) where it is described as "Musik zu einem Puppenspiel" (Music for a puppet play) a title that would be equally valid for many another Keetman piece.

Many possibilities that have so far hardly been considered lie here. By no means least important they can also be made effective through the technical means of film, television and recordings.

SCHULWERK AT THE MOZARTEUM

After an experimental course with a group of children at the Mozarteum, Eberhard Preussner, who had become director of that institution in 1948, engaged Keetman to start regular children's classes in the autumn of 1949. She started with children aged eight to ten years and could now include the important movement training that had not been possible on the radio programmes.

It was a happy coincidence that a former student of the Güntherschule, Traude Schrattenecker, had her own gymnastic and dance studio in Salzburg. Receptive to Keetman's work she made her trained children available for work with the children in the Mozarteum's music classes. Taught at first separately the two groups could soon be combined, so that through the interpenetration of movement and elemental music each child soon caught up with the others in those activities at which they were respectively less experienced. Thus we had created at children's level a parallel type of study with that at the Güntherschule that had had to stop so suddenly.

Both groups were taught intensively, twice weekly, in the fundamentals of elemental music and movement. This included rhythmic exercises, speech exercises, singing, playing instruments (drums, timpani, barred percussion, recorders) improvisation and conducting exercises. In addition they had a movement training that included rhythmic-gymnastic exercises and simple childlike movement games that also, to a great extent included the use of instruments such as tambourines, claves, jingles worn on the ankles and timpani among others. From this activity small dances were created to which Keetman made up music according to the abilities of the children concerned. After a short time these music and movement examples could be shown internally at the Mozarteum.

Invitations soon came for demonstrations in other Austrian music colleges, so that our work was known to a wider circle.

Besides these developments at the Mozarteum the school radio programmes were still continuing. They were the basis for the first books that from 1950 were published by Schott in five volumes — a new chapter in the history of Schulwerk had started. The work was edited volume by volume as it arose from the progressive activity with children and later with adolescents at the Bavarian Radio. The overall title "Music for Children" was retained though some of the pieces in volumes 4 and 5 extend beyond a child's horizon.

Here I quote from Eberhard Preussner, who wrote for the prospectus of the complete edition as follows:

"The main part of Orff-Schulwerk's "Music for Children" is now completed in five volumes. It is a work that Carl Orff over three decades constantly started afresh.

"It makes a decisive contribution to the development of modern music education.

"One cannot value too highly the special fact that it is a composer who has introduced this fundamental reform in the field of music education. This gives it an unusual unity between educational exercise and style of improvisation that makes Orff-Schulwerk a work of reference for the whole of today's music and music education. It also enables progress from the educational to the artistic to be made without a break, or rather that from the very beginning art and education are bound together as one unity, from the simplest pentatonic exercise to the proven art style, in fact to Orff's "Carmina Burana" and "Antigonae". The use of text material shows this same wide range. It reaches from children's rhyme games and fairy stories to old French ballads and to the verse of Goethe and Hölderlin, recited in a way that brings out the sonorities of the language.

This is therefore a demanding production, that not only presupposes the collaboration of the teacher, but also their continuing the work on the basis of these fundamentals. Schulwerk is neither a thread that leads one through the maze nor is it a method that seeks to provide a kind of educational scaffolding, but rather a complete work in which today's music and music education, as it concerns young people, music lovers, professional music teachers and musicians, is anchored.

A fundamental work of the highest imaginative and musical potency."

From "Music for Children"

228

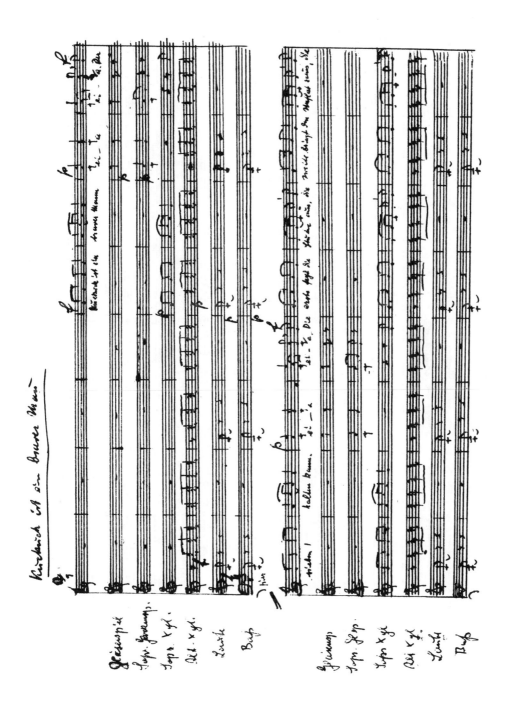

229

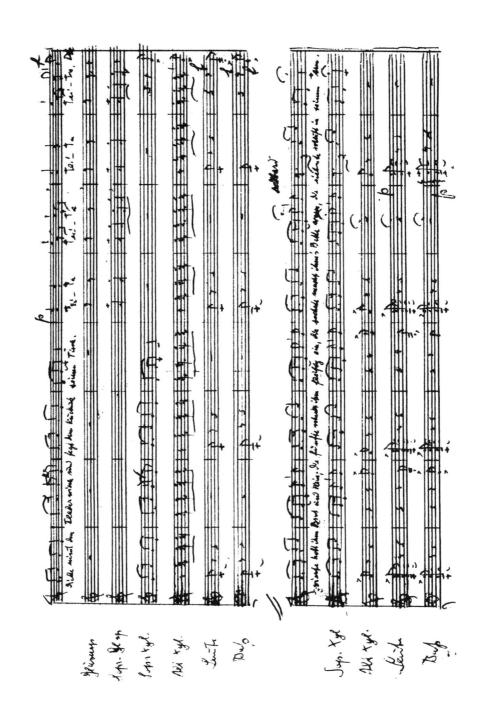

230

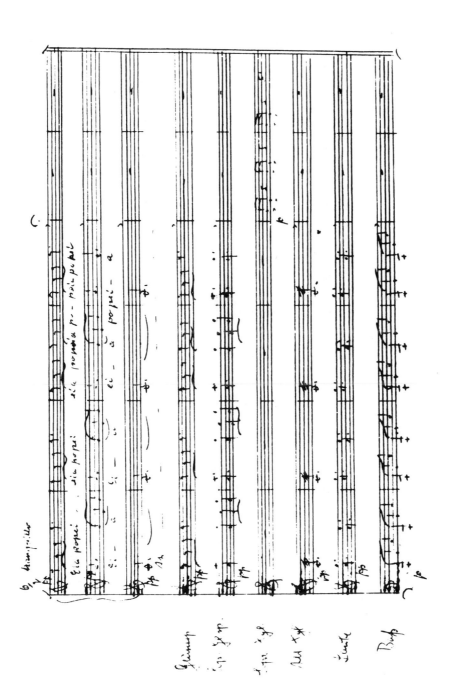

231

Finale: „Goethe, Walpurgisnachttraum"

232

Full details of the contents of the five volumes is unnecessary here for the explanatory notes in the volumes themselves, and later the literature accompanying the gramophone records have given this already. Merely an outline of the five volumes is given here:

Volume I   PENTATONIC
                       Nursery rhymes and songs
                       Rhythmic and melodic exercises I
                       Instrumental pieces

Volume II   MAJOR: DRONE BASS AND TRIADS
                       Drone with six and seven notes
                       Triads I/II and I/VI

Volume III   MAJOR: DOMINANT AND SUBDOMINANT
                       Triad V
                       Other keys
                       Triad IV
                       Sevenths and ninths

Volume IV   MINOR: DRONE BASS AND TRIADS
                       Drone bass: aeolian, dorian, phrygian
                       Triads I/VII, I/III and others

Volume V   MINOR: DOMINANT AND SUBDOMINANT
                       Triad V
                       Triad IV
                       Rhythmic and melodic exersies II
                       Finale

Paul Müller, an old pupil and friend, long since connected with Orff-Schulwerk, that above all brought me in touch with Klaus Becker, came to me one day with the idea of making a film about Schulwerk that was still far too little known by the public in general.

After discussion with the imaginative camera man Heinz Tichawsky, he brought me a draft of the script that seemed to me very suitable. We immediately started with intensive preparations with the children who were thrilled at the prospect of taking part in a film.

Besides the already composed music and movement sequences — a small timpani dance and a solo with claves that consciously referred back to our work at the Güntherschule — we could also include a dance improvisation that developed organically, entirely from conducting movements.

From conducted entry . . .

. . . to movement
improvisation

235

Timpani dance

Since the film was taken just before Easter the thought came to me to use a song like "Winteraustreiben" (Driving Winter Out) and to film it outside in the country so that the whole game had a real connection with the time of year. The penetrating sound of the hurdy-gurdy, that we used here for the first time, was particularly appropriate for work out of doors.

"Winteraustreiben"
"Driving Winter Out"

STARTING OUT IN THE WIDER WORLD

At the occasion of an international conference for music school directors at the Mozarteum Academy in 1953, demonstration lessons given by Keetman with children of different ages were seen by Dr. Arnold Walter, Director of the Royal Conservatory of Music in Toronto, and Prof. Naohiro Fukui, Director of the Musashino Music Academy in Tokyo. Each spontaneously decided to introduce this educational work with elemental music and movement, that was for them quite new, into their own countries. This meant that my ideas had started out into the wider world.

At the instigation of Dr. Walter one of his students, Doreen Hall, studied for a year with Keetman in Salzburg. On her return home she built up Schulwerk in Canada and, together with Dr. Walter, she brought out and published the first version in English.

Prof. Fukui started independently, with the help of the Schulwerk books, to try to effect a transplant of Schulwerk to Japan. Here for the first time the problem of how far Schulwerk could be built into a foreign culture was encountered. Keetman and I, on the study and lecture tour we made in 1962, were able to discover the spontaneity of the Japanese children of all ages, and how they reacted to Schulwerk with enthusiasm and talent, especially to the instruments and to the pentatonic mode, familiar to them of course. We also found how open-minded the teachers were and how naturally this elemental style integrated itself into this foreign music culture. Later the Musashino Music Academy organised its own training centre for Schulwerk teachers.

Meanwhile students at the Mozarteum had begun to be interested in Schulwerk and so Preussner decided from 1953 to arrange courses for Mozarteum students and for those from outside who were interested. This meant yet another approach to the work for Keetman, for these students would be mostly music teachers in the making. There were three students on the first course that were later to have places of significance for Schulwerk: Lotte Flach from Germany, who could soon be appointed as Keetman's helper and colleague and who later became a tutor at the Orff - Institut; Daniel Helldén of Sweden, who after his studies made a Swedish version of the first two Schulwerk volumes; and the Danish Minna Lange, who became Keetman's successor at the Mozarteum and later supplied the Danish edition.

The first Schulwerk records "Music for Children" made in 1956 and 1957 by Columbia/Electrola were important for the further dissemination of the Schulwerk idea. They contained material from the first two Schulwerk volumes. It was at these recordings that Margaret Murray, a musician from London who belonged to the recording team, first became acquainted with Schulwerk. Since Columbia had decided to bring out an English version of these two records, she was given the task of finding corresponding English children's rhymes and speech exercises or of making translations. This marked the beginning of her work on the five volumes of the English Schulwerk edition "Music for Children" and an extended activity as a Schulwerk teacher.

The first Schulwerk film, that was provided with a synchronised commentary, was hired out to interested people all over the world, and the Schulwerk broadcasts of the Bavarian Radio, that were used by many other radio stations, made Schulwerk known to ever wider circles. It now reached in quick succession, Switzerland, Belgium, Holland, Portugal, Yugoslavia, Spain, Latin America, the U.S.A., Turkey, Israel and Greece.

ORFF-SCHULWERK INFORMATION CENTRE AND SEMINAR

The questions asking where one could study Schulwerk in depth, where one could find literature, guidance and information, increased. The short courses that were being held everywhere in the country awoke great interest and made the need for an authentic training centre all the more imperative. Towards the end of 1960 I showed Preussner a proposal of how I imagined such an "Information Centre for Orff-Schulwerk" could be set up, something that I had for a long time thought necessary, and I outlined the scope of functions and activities that I intended: A training centre in which music, movement and speech should be taught with equal emphasis, and a centre that should catch and satisfy the interest and desire for information that was now world-wide.

Preussner agreed with all my suggestions. We only lacked the right personality to whom we could entrust the task of building up such a centre, a task that would be comprehensive and that would require special knowledge. I found such a person in Will Götze.

I had known Götze since the middle 'twenties, the days of Mary Wigman's famous dance evenings. He accompanied her on the piano, and for her dances he wrote music, including percussion, that was original and that caused a sensation at the time. Then he became a Kapellmeister (orchestral conductor) in a theatre and I lost sight of him. After several years I met him again in Frankfurt am Main where he was conducting my Midsummer Night's Dream music. Then in 1949 Eugen Jochum, coming from Hamburg, brought him to the Bavarian Radio in order, with his help, to build up a symphony orchestra. As in his other posts, he again showed his exceptional talent for organisation. He soon became head of the Music Department and work in common brought us together again. In 1951 I was able to interest him in a new series of Schulwerk broadcasts that were now not only for children but also for young adolescents and that we directed together for some time. Since 1958 he had been in retirement and I hoped to gain his services for my Salzburg plans.

Preussner, who up till then had never met Götze, found the right solution. He engaged him as a kind of free-lance colleague, since Götze did not want to be tied in any way.

In the building up of the Information Centre and Seminar Will Götze was my most important helper and of considerable support. Since he had arranged to have an "itinerant office" — no special room was at first available for him — he went about his new work immediately, with energy and singleness of purpose.

Academy for Music and Dramatic Art
in Salzburg

ORFF SCHULWERK
OPENING OF
INFORMATION CENTRE AND SEMINAR

Monday, 15th July 1961, 10.00 a.m., Wiener Saal
Welcoming address: President Dr. Eberhard Preussner
Speech by Herrn Bundesministers für Unterricht
Dr. Heinrich Drimmel

Lectures and Demonstrations

Monday, 10th July	Lecture by Dr. Werner Thomas, Heidelberg
10.30, Wiener Saal	"Orff-Schulwerk — a pedagogical province?"
11.30, Grosser Saal	Demonstration by children from the Suse Böhm Dance Studio, Munich "First stages of Orff-Schulwerk"
15.00 Wiener Saal	Lecture Dr. Raoul Schindler, Vienna "The Psychological Foundations of Music and Movement"
16.00 Wiener Saal	Lecture by Dr. Karl Hofmarksrichter, Director for the Institute for the Deaf and Dumb, Straubing "Rhythmic Education with Deaf and Dumb Children" followed by film "Deaf children make music" (Orff-Schulwerk)

Tuesday, 11th July	Lecture by Dr. Werner Thomas, Heidelberg
10.00, Wiener Saal	"Orff-Schulwerk as Model" Examples from the Schulwerk work of different lands (recorded tapes and records)
Wednesday, 12th July 15.00 Grosser Saal	Demonstration by choir and instrumental groups of the Mozarteum Academy, conducted by Gunild Keetman
Thursday, 13th July	Lecture by Dr. Werner Thomas, Heidelberg
10.00 Wiener Saal	"Resounding Language" Call — Rhyme — Saying — Poem (with recorded tapes and records)

In the autumn of 1961 the regular training at the Seminar, for which four semesters were planned, was started. Together with Keetman I took over the direction. Further teachers were: Lotte Flach, Barbara Haselbach, Traude Schrattenecker; in addition Franz Tenta came from the Mozarteum to give recorder lessons and Rudolf Schingerlin took all the percussion.

Soon Wilhelm Keller, who had been familiar with Orff-Schulwerk for some time, was appointed director to relieve me, and was also responsible for all theoretical subjects. He had previously been lecturing in music education at the Pädagogischen Hochschule (Teacher Training College) in Lüneburg.

The students were taught, as were the very well attended children's classes, in subsidiary rooms of the already overfilled Mozarteum. Because of the ever-increasing numbers of students and the resulting lack of space it was decided to set up a new building for the "Orff-Institut" in the grounds of Schloss Frohnburg, Salzburg. This to be managed with the support of the Austrian Ministry of Education, and by the town and the region of Salzburg. The new building was to have four large teaching rooms, a larger number of smaller rooms for individual lessons and small ensembles, and apart from this a library, a workshop for making instruments, rest rooms and a secretarial office.

It was thanks to the energetic involvement of the then Minister for Education. Dr. Heinrich Drimmel, the then Finance minister Dr.

Josef Klaus and the then Sektionsrat Dr. Erwin Thalhammer, that the building could start at once. Together with Preussner they made a unique Quadrivium.

For the international furtherance of Orff-Schulwerk, both idealistically and materially, a society was founded in December 1961 called "Förderer des Orff-Schulwerks" with Dr. h.c. Manfred Mautner-Markhof, Vienna, as president. The founding of a German branch of this society followed under the presidency of Dr. Ernst von Siemens on 18th June, 1962 in Munich.

The publishing of Orff-Institut Year Books in the following years was an important step. They not only included information and reports, but also articles by well-known authors on the widest variety of subjects.

Dr. Werner Thomas, in collaboration with Will Götze, brought out three year books published by Schott during the years 1962 - 1968. The first also came out in an English version and the third appeared in edited form in both Japanese and Russian. As head of a gymnasium (a school for children of secondary age) in Ludwigshafen, Dr. Thomas had taught Schulwerk for many years. For many years he had also given Schulwerk a theoretic and scientific foundation through his articles and commentaries and as a philologist he had particularly brought out the language component.

Thomas draws attention to the importance of the year books in his preface to the first one. "The articles in the 1962 Year Book are like a commentary to the text."

Apart from the Year Books the Orff-Institut has published, under the editorship of Lilo Gersdorf, a series of booklets called "Informationen", that have appeared at random intervals.

The first working conference arranged by the Orff-Institut took place from 26th - 29th April, 1962, at the Mozarteum Academy and it was called "Orff-Schulwerk in the school."

The conference began with an introductory lecture from Preussner, and there followed demonstrations, lectures and discussions. Many pedagogues from at home and abroad were present.

Lectures and reports from the conference were partly printed in the year books, as was my appeal "Schulwerk Past and Future" that is given here in extracts:

"Year in, year out, many Schulwerk courses are given for teachers of all kinds. Schulwerk is taught alongside other subjects in various schools of music, in schools for gymnastics and dance, and in private courses. Useful as all these efforts may be, they do not alter the fact that Schulwerk has not yet found the place where it belongs, the place where it can be most effective and where there is the possibility of continuous and progressive work, and where its connections with other subjects can be explored, developed and fully exploited. This place is the school. 'Music for Children' is for the school.

"Because I do not wish to speak technically about all the questions of educational reform that are being discussed so much in all parts of the world today, I should like to express my thoughts in an untechnical way that should be easy to understand. For this we must return again to Nature. Elementary music, word and movement, play, everything that awakens and develops the powers of the spirit, this is the 'humus' of the spirit, the humus without which we face the danger of a spiritual erosion.

"When does erosion occur in Nature? When the land is wrongly exploited; for instance, when the natural water supply is disturbed through too much cultivation, or when, for utilitarian reasons, forests and hedges fall as victims of drawing-board mentality; in short, when the balance of nature is lost by interference. In the same way I would like to repeat: Man exposes himself to spiritual erosion if he estranges himself from his elementary essentials and thus loses his balance.

"Just as humus in nature makes growth possible, so elementary music gives to the child powers that cannot otherwise come to fruition. It is at the primary school age that the imagination must be stimulated; and opportunities for emotional development, which contain experience of the ability to feel, and the power to control the expression of that feeling, must also be provided.

Everything that a child of this age experiences, everything in him that has been awakened and nurtured is a determining factor for the whole of his life. Much can be destroyed at this age that can never be regained, much can remain undeveloped that can never be reclaimed."

My repeated appeals and manifestos did not go unheeded. At home and abroad cells grew that took up the idea and the work and carried it further, and that have already produced a comprehensive literature about Schulwerk.

A series of model classes in elementary schools were instituted in various schools, in particular in Bavaria (at the instigation of Prof. Handerer, Pädagogische Hochschule, Regensburg) and Berlin (through Margot Schneider, Carl-Orff-Grundschule Wilmersdorf). The teachers chosen for these classes were given time off by their respective regional authorities to study for two years at the Orff-Institut.

In America, too, experiments that were laid out on a big scale were started with Schulwerk in schools (Bellflower Project among others). In many countries Orff-Schulwerk societies were started out of the need to exchange experiences and to obtain information.

A special contribution to public appearances was made by Suse Böhm with her children's dance studio in Munich, a school that based their teaching entirely on Orff-Schulwerk. They appeared in performances, demonstrations, took part in films and television, and were the subject of a picture book.

THE ORFF-INSTITUT

*"We always stand at the beginning. Now I
know well that I am only placing a feeble
piece of coal in damp, wet straw, but I see a
wind, and it is not far away, it will blow on
the coal, the wet straw around me will
gradually dry, and then become warm, then
catch fire and then burn. As wet as it is
around me, it will burn, it will burn"*

Pestalozzi

Within a year of commencement the new building of the
Orff-Institut was so far advanced that we were able to take
possession on 25th October 1963.

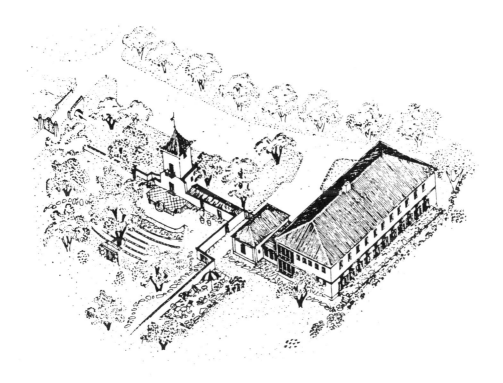

Sketch by Architect Dr. Helmut Sylvester Keidel — Salzburg
The new school building of the Orff-Institut on the southern boundary of
Schloss Frohnburg, Salzburg

AKADEMIE FÜR MUSIK UND DARSTELLENDE KUNST „MOZARTEUM"
IN SALZBURG

Freitag, den 25. Oktober 1963, 11 Uhr

Feierstunde

im Musiksaal des Schlosses Frohnburg anläßlich der

Einweihung des Orff-Institutes

an der Akademie „Mozarteum"

Zur Einleitung:

Carl Orff   Aus „Carmina Burana"

                       Ecce gratum

                       In trutina

                       Were diu werlt alle min

             Bläser der Akademie „Mozarteum"
             Leitung: Kurt Prestel

Begrüßung: Professor Dr. Eberhard Preussner,
             Präsident der Akademie „Mozarteum"

Ansprachen: Bürgermeister Kommerzialrat Alfred Bäck
             Landesrat Josef Kaut
             Sektionsrat Dr. Erwin Thalhammer
             Dr. h. c. Carl Orff

Anschließend Weihe des Institutes durch Hochwürden Herrn Prälaten Dr. Karl Berg
und Hochwürden Herrn Stadtpfarrer Josef Tomaschek

Führung durch das Institut durch Herrn Architekten Professor Dr. Helmut Sylvester
Keidel und Herrn Technischen Rat Stadtbaumeister Felix Ennemoser

My speech on that occasion began with the words:

"With all the joy in the new home that we now have for the Institut, and over the unique working rooms, there steals over me a sense of oppression when I think of the task that lies before me, that is yet to be accomplished. A task that grows in size the more one tackles it. The far-reaching plan of how our work will develop is, as far as possible clear to me. The sustaining ideas lie in time and I hope so to drive the development forward that I can hand the work over to my successors and young teachers.

"All my ideas, the ideas of an elemental music education are not new. It was only given to me to present these old, imperishable ideas in todays terms, to make them come alive for us. I do not feel like the creator of something new, but more like someone who passes on an old inheritance, or like a relay runner who lights his torch at the fires of the past and brings it into the present.

"This will also be the lot of my successors, for if the idea remains alive it will not be bound by their mortality. Remaining alive also means to change with time and through time. Therein lies the hope and the excitement."

Hand in hand with the external building the internal one was also progressing. New teachers were appointed, teaching schemes worked at, changed, renewed, aims formulated and in addition to the seminar, training courses and conferences at home and abroad were given.

The training in the seminar should enable the student to use the means and method of Elemental Music and Movement Training according to Orff-Schulwerk principles in nursery school (pre-school), in general and further education institutions, in professional music and movement studies and also in social and medical training. The Institut's children's classes are available to the students for teaching practice.

A significant step in the development of the Institut was the appointment of Dr. Hermann Regner as its Director. He had previously directed the Seminar for Youth and Folk Music at the

Hochschulinstitut for Music in Trossingen with Orff-Schulwerk as a central subject. At the invitation of "Pro Arte Brasil" he introduced Schulwerk into Brazil through courses in Rio de Janeiro, Brasilia, Sao Paulo and Teresepolis. Regner took over the Seminar training at the Orff-Institut, and in addition he was active and conscientious in his approach to countless lectures, demonstrations, courses and seminars in the most varied parts of the world.

Next to Dr. Regner, Barbara Haselbach became a leading force. After studying German Philology and Musicology she completed a dance training with Harald Kreutzberg, Mary Wigman's master pupil. She learnt about Orff-Schulwerk from Keetman and with increasing responsibilities she took over the whole movement department to which she brought much new impetus. Like Regner she was instrumental in spreading information through many important courses at home and abroad.

Wilhelm Keller pledged himself from the beginning to the use of Schulwerk with handicapped children and gained many rewards in this field. In addition to his Seminar teaching he gave many lectures and courses, particularly in Eastern Europe. He has been made Director of the Institut for Musical Social and Medical Education. In this area Schulwerk is opening up new spheres of activity that have only just begun.

The remaining tutors at the Institute have also given frequent courses all over the world and Schulwerk teachers from abroad have come to visit the Orff Institut. This fruitful exchange has brought new impulses and stimulus to the work.

The protective hand of the Mozarteum's President, my friend Eberhard Preussner, lay over it all. Without him the Orff-Institut would never have been built.

And then there came the faithful, tireless Will Götze as helper, adviser, and rescuer in all the difficult situations and dangers that such a very extensive undertaking brings with it.

MUSICA POETICA

The five main Orff-Schulwerk volumes presented no definitive conclusion. Over the years many supplementary books have appeared with practice pieces for individual instruments such as xylophone, timpani and brass. Apart from this the volumes from the old Schulwerk editions such as those for piano and violin, and some books for percussion and recorder, have appeared in newly edited forms. In addition a series called "Lieder für die Schule" has appeared, that comprises folk songs in settings with simple instrumentation that correspond to the principles of Orff-Schulwerk.

Through the initiative of Dr. Alfred Krings and Rudolf Ruby from the firm Harmonia Mundi, recordings were made during the years 1963 - 75. These took place under the artistic direction of Keetman and myself and presented an authentic documentation of Schulwerk in sound. The recordings began in May 1963 with the separate work, already mentioned, the "Weihnachtsgeschichte" (Christmas Story).

In the course of the following thirteen years ten records were produced in random order, each with a detailed commentary by Dr. Werner Thomas. The contents of the ten records correspond to the arrangement of material in the five main Schulwerk volumes, but also contain material from the supplementary volumes and some newly-composed vocal and instrumental pieces. The development of the speech exercise in various forms is new, and so is the frequent realisation of the oft repeated demand in the "Notes" of the volumes, that the pieces be extended in terms of form and instrumentation. These records are a documentation of twenty years Schulwerk experience. An impressive as well as an internationally understandable title had to be found for them. "Musica Poetica" speaks for itself and includes poetry without having to go back to the meaning of this term in musical history. The title emphasises that in the preparation of Schulwerk material for the series of records the word — from ancient children's rhymes to the poetry of Sophocles, Goethe and Hölderlin — acquired more and more significance.

At this time a supplementary volume called "Paralipomena" — that means a collection of things left out and overlooked, was published, and this contained a selection of pieces newly composed for the record series and also some pieces that seemed fundamental but had not yet been published.

Two further volumes "Stücke für Sprechchor" (1969) (Pieces for choir of speakers) and Stücke für Sprecher, Sprechchor und Schlagwerk" (1976) (Pieces for speaker, choir of speakers and percussion) that finally leave the realm of Schulwerk behind. They are a compendium of different kinds of speech forms, solo and choral, with and without supporting and characterising instrumental accompaniment. They widen the horizon of the educational work and can be understood as a signpost to free artistic work. Although these pieces appear to be the furthest removed from the starting point of Schulwerk it should not be overlooked that a big arc stretches from the first speech experiments to one's own accompaniment on a drum as in the early days of the Güntherschule (see p. 23 ff) to these end forms of speech compositions. For work with young people and adults, and also in drama schools they can offer new material.

These two volumes represent the end of my contribution to Schulwerk as a composer, in so far as one can talk about an end at all in this context.

From „Stücken für Sprecher, Sprechchor und Schlagwerk"

Das Ölfeld
(Bert Brecht)

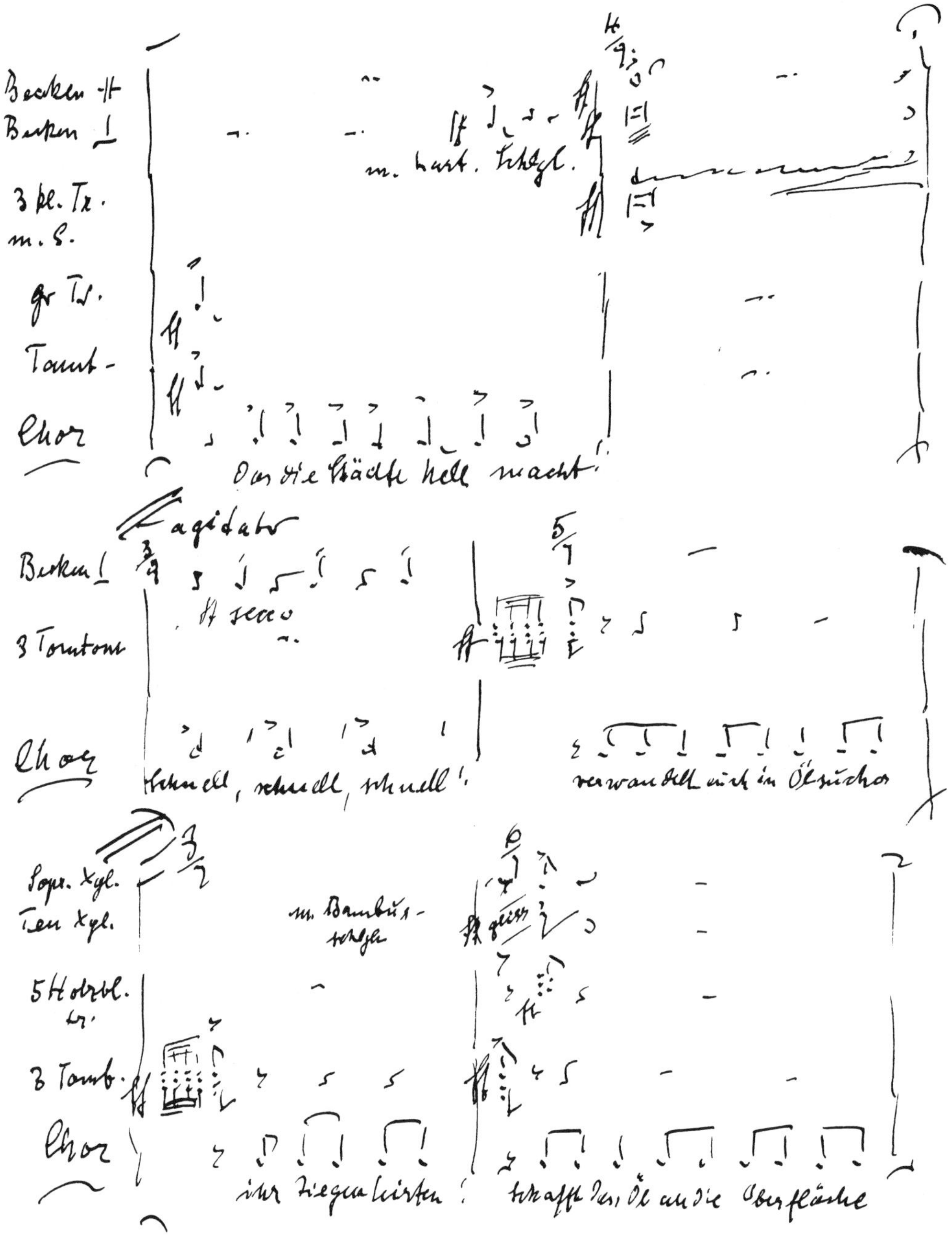
Chor
Das die Städte hell macht!
agitato
Chor
schnell, schnell, schnell!
verwandelt euch in Ölsucher
Chor
ihr Ziegenhirten!
schafft das Öl an die Oberfläche

255

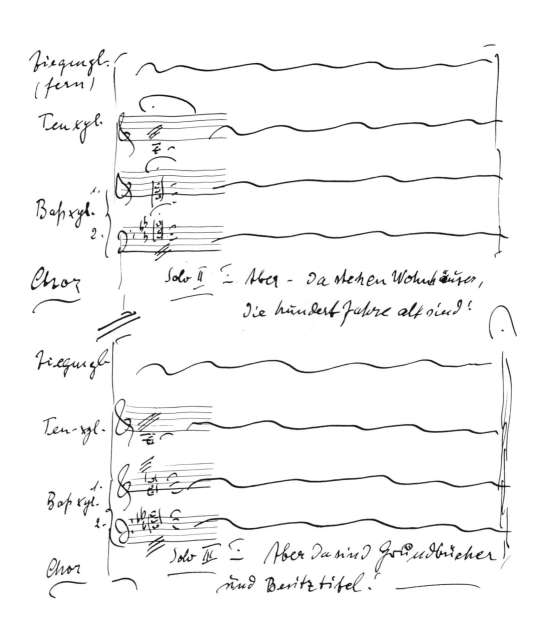

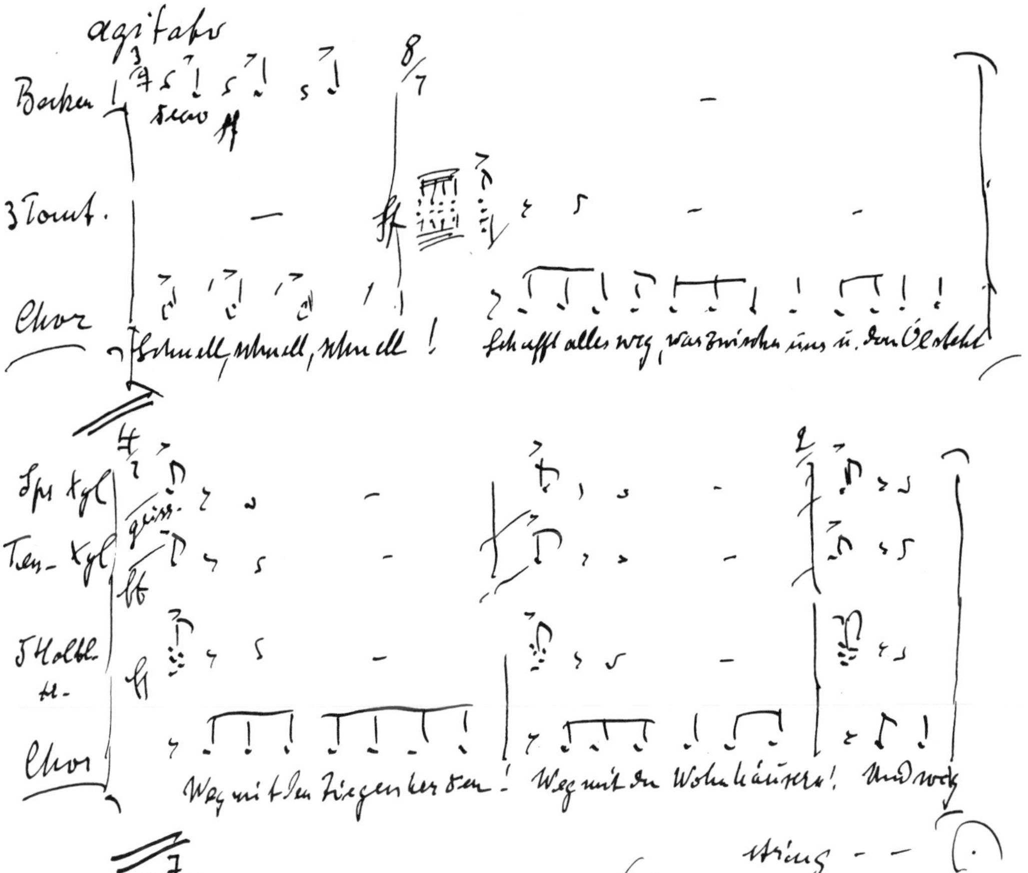
agitato
Chor
Schnell, schnell, schnell!
Sopr Xyl
Ten Xyl
gliss.
Chor
Weg mit den Wohnhäusern! Und weg
Sopr Xyl
Ten Xyl
Chor
mit den Grundbüchern u. Besitz-titeln!

258

The Oil Field

Here is oil! Oil is here! It's lying here,
Makes the motors run, which sets the ships in motion!
Cylinder-lubricating oil lies here in the ground!
Which makes the city bright! Quickly!
Turn yourselves into oil seekers, you goatherds! Quickly!
Bring the oil to the surface, carry away the rocks, bore
The ground, you farmers!

But there are goats grazing on those fields!
But hundred-year-old houses stand there!
But there are claims to the ground and title deeds!

Quickly! Away with all obstacles between us and the oil!
Away with the goats! Away with the houses!
And away with the ground claims and title deeds!
Here is oil! Oil is here!
Cylinder-lubricating oil is here,
And it makes the cities bright!

From "Pieces for speaker, speech choir and percussion"

The Frohnburg

THE FROHNBURG

Schloss Frohnburg, once the property of the titled family, von Kuenburg, is situated on the Allee, an avenue, that leads to Schloss Hellbrunn. It stands in a large park and has extensive accommodation. After many years of continuous pressure by Preussner and other personalities from Salzburg's musical life, it was at last acquired from the Austrian State, and in 1957 it was opened as a residential hostel for the students of the Mozarteum Academy. Thus another concert hall had been gained. Since 1961, the year of the founding of the Seminar and Information Centre for Orff-Schulwerk, we were able to hold our International Summer Courses there. The open-air theatre by the "Trompeterturm" (trumpeter's tower) was prepared as a studio theatre for the opera school of the Mozarteum.

"Astutuli", rehearsal

Placed so near the buildings of the Orff-Institut it offered us the attractive possibility of studying drama and including it in our studies, which had always been part of my plan.

Elemental music impels towards scenic presentation, towards theatre.

Since the open-air theatre was a favourite of Preussner's we decided to prepare a performance for his sixty-fifth birthday that would involve everyone at the Institut. My Bavarian comedy "Astutuli" was an obvious choice, a piece for the theatre with many small roles and choruses of speakers, singers and dancers. Only the roles of the Gagler and the Sterzer would be reserved for professional actors unless there was a special natural talent available. To find players for the percussion orchestra would give us no trouble. This, our first attempt at practical collaboration with the seminars for drama and stage scenery at the Mozarteum worked out to mutual advantage and the study and preparation of the work showed positive educational results.

AKADEMIE FÜR MUSIK UND DARSTELLENDE KUNST
«MOZARTEUM» IN SALZBURG

ORFF-INSTITUT

Freilichtbühne Schloß Frohnburg
Samstag, 30. Mai 1964, 20.30 Uhr, und Sonntag, 31. Mai 1964, 20.30 Uhr,

Carl Orff

Astutuli

Eine bairische Komödie

Es treten auf:

Zween Landsterzer	Gerhard Zemann Manfred Böldl
Zween Burger	Ronald Rauch Branko Samarovski
Jörg Zaglstecher, der Burgermeister . . .	Haavard Seeböck
Seine Tochter Fundula	Ulrike Fischer
Vellicula / Hortula Gespielinnen	Heidrun Herzog Wulfried Fischer
Drei Sponsierer	Volker Deutsch Peter Schwab Raimund Gensel
Die vom hochweisen Rat	Bernd Meyer zur Heide Achim Dünnwald Henning Rühle
Wunibald Hirnstößl, der Wachter	Loris Z. Tjeknavorian
Der fremde Gagler	Dominik Bisjak
Die Fahrende	Barbara Haselbach
Burger einer kleinen Stadt, Männer und Weiberleut, Alte und Junge	Barbara Holzach Irmgard Kieber Sabine Lattermann Christine Oakley Gertraud Peer Erika Prümm Johanna Reutter Gerlinde Russinger Sieglinde Vogel Daniel Basi Klaus Hochmann Norbert Meder

Die Stori begibt sich vor undenklicher Zeit

Es spielen:

Danae Apostolidou, Dagmar Bauz, Margit Cronmüller, Renate Dänel,
Ana Domingues, Knut Elsenwenger, Dagmar Emmig, Lotte Flach,
Friedrun Gerheuser, Wilhelm Keller, Gerhard Laber, Wilma McCool,
Joana Silva, Saundra Skyhar, Harry Smaller

Beleuchter: Fritz Gehbauer   Inspizient: Traude Schrattenecker
Szenenbild und Kostüme:
Studierende der Bühnenbildklasse HEINZ BRUNO GALLEE
Musikalische Leitung: KURT PRESTEL
Inszenierung: CLAUS THOMAS

265

That evening we talked a long time with Preussner and discussed the production, a model in its way and a promising beginning. We indulged in fantastic future plans, filled with the new possibilities that now offered themselves.

In the rooms of the Institut this auspicious start was celebrated till far into the night. In the circle of lecturers and tutors Preussner gave a fiery speech about the plans for the further extension of the Institut. He was in radiant mood and spoke with unbroken optimism and captivating charm. Impetus and control were as one. —

Who could have foreseen that it was his farewell greeting, as it were. A few weeks later I was sitting by his sick-bed.

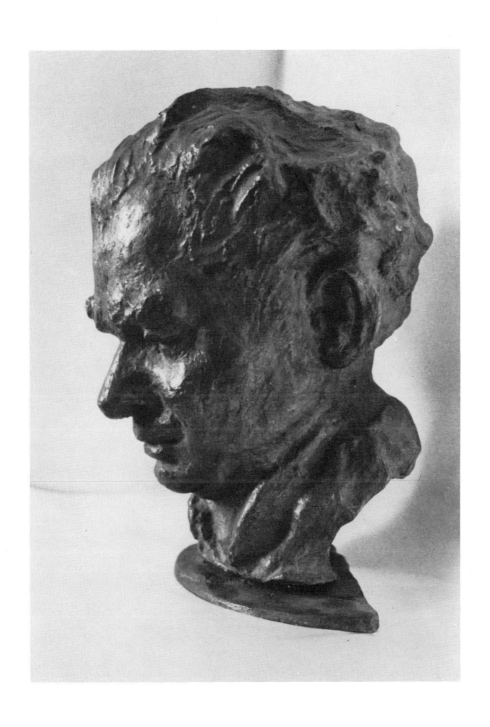

Ave atque vale —

In October 1970 the extension to the Orff-Institut, that Preussner had initiated, was started. Through it the Orff-Institut acquired a library of its own, a large room for dance and a long-needed lecture hall and theatre, as well as additional teaching and rest rooms.

Orff-Institut Salzburg, extension
Design: Prof. Dr. Helmut Sylvester Keidel, Salzburg

Since the founding of the Information Centre in 1961, the development of the Orff-Institut and the Schulwerk work at home and abroad has been continuously documented in the Orff-Institut's Year Books and in their publication "Informationen", in films and in many publications and reports at home and abroad. A detailed presentation in this context is therefore unnecessary.

FROM THE WORK AT THE ORFF-INSTITUT

Old music: Crumhorns and Racket (Franz Tenta)

Old dance forms

Percussion ensemble

Tubular bells, xylophone, metallophone, gong

Orchestra and choir rehearsal directed by Hermann Regner

Movement teaching with Barbara Haselbach

Studies in movement . . .

. . . and jumping

273

Movement studies: Tension

IN RETROSPECT

In all our many and varied experiments with elemental music, that have lasted for over half a century, nothing has actually become outdated. The elemental remains a foundation that is timeless. The elemental always means a new beginning. Whatever they may be, the fashionable attributes that can and do attach themselves to all work must fall off again. Everything up to date, conditioned by time, becomes out of date. In its timelessness the elemental finds understanding all over the world. So it was not Schulwerk, about which I have written here in order to record an idea, but the idea itself that went round the world.

The elemental is always reproductive. I am glad that I was destined to seize the reproductive spark, to accost the elemental in mankind and to awaken the spirit that binds us together.

The Symposium ''Orff-Schulwerk 75'' in Salzburg, in the way it brought together people from the furthest regions and lands, was the best proof of this. It was not only a meeting, a getting to know one another for the first time, but, as it were, a refinding of one another in mutual understanding.

So I would like at this juncture to say thank-you to my friends, colleagues and helpers all over the world, a thank-you that they may experience again in the success of their work.

The Orff-Institut, 1976

APPENDIX

CHRONOLOGY

1924   Güntherschule founded in Munich by Dorothee Günther and Carl Orff

1925   Maja Lex comes to the Güntherschule

1926   Gunild Keetman comes to the Güntherschule

1928   Karl Maendler builds the first xylophones for the Güntherschule

1930   First public appearance of the dance group, performances at home and abroad

1931   First publications: "Orff-Schulwerk — Elementare Musikübung" in collaboration with Gunild Keetman

1932   First meeting with Eberhard Preussner and Leo Kestenberg

1933   Branch of the Güntherschule established in Berlin (formerly Trümpy-Schule)

1936   Involvement in the Festival "Olympic Youth" on the occasion of the eleventh Olympic Games in Berlin

1944   Compulsory closing of the Güntherschule

1945   Bombing of the Güntherschule buildings and resultant loss of instruments and archives; end of the Güntherschule

1948   Beginning of the Schulwerk programmes on Bayerischer Rundfunk (Bavarian Radio); "The Christmas Story"

1949   Studio 49 founded by Klaus Becker
        Schulwerk courses for children at the Mozarteum taken by Gunild Keetman

1950   Start of "Musik für Kinder" (Music for Children) publications

1953   Schulwerk demonstrations at the International Conference of Directors of Music Academies at the Mozarteum Academy; first contact with people from abroad

1954   Last publication "Musik für Kinder" (Music for Children) Book V
        First Schulwerk Film called "Musik für Kinder" and "Music for Children"

1956/57	First recordings in German and English of "Music for Children" I and II (Columbia-Electrola)
1957/58	Schulwerk television series at Bayerischer Rundfunk (Bavarian Radio) taken by Gunild Keetman and Godela Orff
1958	Guest courses and demonstrations (Gunild Keetman) abroad (Belgium, Switzerland and Italy)
1961	Founding Seminar and Information Centre for Orff-Schulwerk at the Mozarteum Academy in Salzburg
	First International Summer Course in the Frohnburg
	Founding the Society "Förderer des Orff-Schulwerks" in Salzburg
1962	First course abroad through tutors from the Orff Institute in Toronto/Canada; "Special Conference on Elementary Music Education — Orff-Schulwerk" in the presence of Carl Orff and Gunild Keetman
	Four weeks lecture and demonstration tour of Japan at the invitation of State Japanese Radio and Television NHK (Orff, Keetman)
	First publication of Orff-Institut Year Books (Jahrbücher)
	New building for the Orff-Institut started
1963	Working Conference "Orff-Schulwerk in the school" at the Mozarteum
	Recording of the "Weihnachtsgeschichte" (Christmas Story) (harmonia mundi)
	Start of the series of "Musica Poetica" recordings (harmonia mundi) completed 1975
	Opening of the Orff-Institut
1964	Filming the "Weihnachtsgeschichte" (Christmas Story)
	First performance of "Astutuli" by students at the Orff-Institut at the open-air theatre of the Frohnburg
	Eberhard Preussner†
1970	Opening the extension to the Orff-Institut
1973	Opening the Institute for Music Therapy at the Orff-Institut, directed by Wilhelm Keller
1975	"Symposium Orff-Schulwerk 1975" at the Orff-Institut

SCHULWERK EDITIONS

German Editions

ORFF-SCHULWERK
ELEMENTARE MUSIKÜBUNG
1930—34

A 1 Rhythmisch-melodische Übung 1. u. 2. Teil (Orff)
B 1 Übung für Schlagwerk: Handtrommel (Bergese)
B 2 Übung für Schlagwerk: Pauken (Bergese)
C 1 Stücke zum Singen und Spielen (Bergese)
D 1 Übung für Stabspiele: Xylophon (Bergese)
E 1 Spielstücke für kleines Schlagwerk (Bergese)
E 2 Spielstücke für kleines Schlagwerk (Keetman)
F 1 Kleines Flötenbuch 1 (Keetman)
F 2 Kleines Flötenbuch 2 (Keetman)
G 1 Spielstücke für Blockflöten (Keetman)
H 1 Spielstücke für Blockflöten u. kl. Schlagwerk (Keetman)
J 1 Tanz- und Spielstücke: Auftakt und Bolero (Keetman)
J 2 Tanz (Keetman)
J 3 Ekstatischer Tanz, Nachtlied (Keetman)
Klavierübung 1: Kleines Spielbuch (Orff)
Klavierübung 2: Üb- und Spielstücke (Bergese)
Klavierübung 3: Üb- und Spielstücke (Bergese)
Kalvierübung 6: Kleine Tänze (Bergese)
Geigenübung 1: Spiel- und Tanzstücke für eine Geige (Orff)
Geigenübung 2: Spiel- u. Tanzstücke für zwei Geigen (Orff)
Alte und neue Tänze für Blockflöten und Handtrommel (Bergese)

Wilhelm Twittenhoff: Grundlagen und Aufbau des Orff-Schulwerks 1935

All of the volumes of the First Edition of the Schulwerk are out of print. A new edition of Volumes E2, G1, H1, Kalvierübung 1, Geigenübung 1 and 2 were issued after 1948.

CARL ORFF — GUNILD KEETMAN
MUSIK FÜR KINDER
1950—54

Volume I   *Im Fünftonraum*
                  Reime und Spiellieder
                  Kuckuck — Sieh Beck — Ringel, Ringel, Reiha — Unk, unk, unk — Wellemännele im Mond — Geht ein Männerl über Land — Der Tag is schon uma — Mädle, tu's Lädle zu — Tromm, tromm, tromm — Reiter zu Pferd — Klopfe, klopfe Ringelchen — O großmächtige Sunne — Stab aus, Stab aus — Drei Wolken am Himmel — Kuckuck ist ein braver Mann — Bumfallera

Rhythmisch-melodische Übung 1
Rhythmen zum Klatschen, Melodieenbauen und Textieren —
Ostinate Begleitrhythmen — Rhythmische Rondospiele und
Kanons — Ostinatoübung für Stabspiele u. a.
Spielstücke

Volume II

Dur: Bordun und Stufen

Bordun im Sechstonraum

Schlaf, Kindlein schlaf — Tanz, Mädchen tanz — Jungfer in dem
roten Rock — Es gingen drei Bauern — Sankt Martin war ein
milder Mann

Bordun im Siebentonraum

Lügenmärchen — Sipp, sapp, seppe — Ahî nu kumet uns diu zît
— Dormi Jesu, mater ridet — Ich leb, weiß nit wie lang — Ich
wünsch dir eine gute Nacht — Es saßen drei Narren

Stufen
Die erste und die zweite Stufe

Kommt und laßt uns tanzen, springen — Sommerkanon — Wie
früh ist auf Sankt Martine — Zwei Spielstücke

Die erste und die sechste Stufe
Die Marterwoch laß still vergehn — Gloria

Volume III

Dur: Dominanten
Die fünfte Stufe

's bunkad Manderl — Die Bernauerin — Carillon de Vendôme —
Der Herr, der schickt den Jockel aus — Die Ammenuhr — Hajo,
hajo, wären wir do

Andere Tonarten

Sur le pont d'Avignon — Guten Morgen, Spielmann —
Rätselspiel — Der Maien ist kommen

Die vierte Stufe

Gassenhauer — Der Wind, der weht — Einzug — Eia, eia, Ostern
ist da — Sunnwend

Mit Septen und Nonen

Rundadinella — Mater et filia — Ennstaler Polka — Zwiefache u.
andere Taktwechseltänze

Volume IV

Moll: Bordun
Aeolisch

Bet' Kinder, bet' — Ein Wahrheitslied — C'était Anne de Bretagne
— Marmotte — Gjeite Lok — Amor, amor — Der jüngste Tag — Es
ist die wunderschönste Brück — Käuzlein — Kukuk hat sich zu
todt gefall'n — Urlicht

Dorisch

Martin liber herre mein — Fröhlicher Ostergesang — Pastourelles — C'est le mai — Wessobrunner Gebet — Morgensegen — Abendsegen — Haussegen — Das Nachthorn — Winteraustreiben und Sommergewinn

Phrygisch

Mutter, ach Mutter, es hungert mich — Die arme Bettelfrau singt das kranke Kind in Schlaf — Märchensprüche — Isegrims Begräbnis — Passion — Himmelfahrt

Stufen

Die erste und die siebente Stufe

Liebe Mutter 's wird finster — Ruhe in Gottes Hand — Es saß ein edly maget schon — Der Feigenbaum

Die erste und dritte und andere Stufen

Bienensegen — Mariae Geburt — Flachssegen — Umspielte Terzen — Es geht ein dunckle Wolcken rein — Es sungen drey engel — Nun singet all — Zum Beschluß

Volume V

Moll: Dominanten

Die fünfte Stufe ohne Leitton

La légende de St. Nicolas — Der faule Schäfer — Johann, spann an — Großmutter Schlangenköchin — Herr Olof

Die fünfte Stufe mit Leitton

La Pénitence de Marie-Madeleine — Am Weyhnachtabend — Villancico: Baile de Nadal — Quand Biron voulut danser — Zu Maien, zu Maien — Konstruktion der Welt

Die vierte Stufe

Lamento — Aria, Komm Trost der Nacht' — Carillon — Berceuse — Des herzen sluzzelin — Vom Schlaraffenland — Das Pfingst-Ei — Chaconne — Entre le boeuf et l'âne gris

Zum Beschluß

Incipiunt Laudes Creaturarum (Sonnengesang) — Jubilationes — Drei Stücke aus dem Wunderhorn

Rhythmisch-melodische Übung II

Sprechstücke

Klein-Flöhchen und Klein-Läuschen — Drei Stücke aus Goethes Faust — Der Chor aus Sophokles' Antigonae (Hölderlin)

Rezitativ

Und es waren Hirten — An dem österlichen Tag — Dialogus Quem queritis in sepulcro' — Media vita

Finale

Aus Goethes Faust: Walpurgisnachtstraum

The titles listed present one of the choices from the previous volumes. The instrumental pieces contained in each volume are not displayed.

Paralipomena

I

Meisenruf — Blaue, blaue Wolken — Ene bene Bohnenblatt — Ist gar ein schöner Garten — Frau Holda — Sitzt an Engerl an der Wand — Der Müller thut mahlen — Geschichtete Ostinati — Nüna, nüna Puppala schlof — Drei kleine Nachspiele — Vier Sprechstücke: Duck dich, Vivos voco, Kommt Zeit, kommt Rat, Schnepfenregel — Schau grad wias regna tuat — Havele Hahne

II

Intrada für Pauken und Trompeten — Ballade vom Herrn Latour — C'était Anne de Bretagne — Geschichtete Ostinati — Abendlied — Vor der Ernte — Der Tod — Zum Einschlafen zu singen — Der Mensch — Zwei Chorsätze: Te lucis ante terminum, Treś magi

III lydisch

Von der Geburt des Herrn — Das arm Kind — Lydisches Flötenstück

IV mixolydisch

Geschichtete Ostinati — Der Meien — Der Froschkönig — Der Eiserne Heinrich — Wiegenlied beim Mondschein zu singen — Das himmlische Leben

Die Weihnachtsgeschichte (The Christmas Story)

Text: Carl Orff
Musik: Gunild Keetman
1948

The text is available in English, Swedish, Dutch and Flemish and in various German dialects.

CARL ORFF
STÜCKE FÜR SPRECHCHOR
1969

Chor aus ‚Oedipus auf Kolonos' (Sophokles-Hölderlin) — Pindars Erste Olympische Hymne (Hölderlin) — An den Schlaf (Sophokles, Philoktetes) — Aus ‚Brot und Wein' (Hölderlin) — Die Jahreszeiten (Hölderlin) — Quando conveniunt — Sentencia — Die frühen Gräber, Weihtrunk an die toten Freunde (Zwei Oden von Klopstock) — Requiem (Hebbel) — Der Abend (Schiller) — Omnia tempus habent — Drei Stücke aus Goethes Faust: Wie traurig steigt die unvollkommne Scheibe, Hexen-Einmal-Eins, Die grauen Weiber

CARL ORFF
STÜCKE FÜR SPRECHER, SPRECHCHOR UND SCHLAGWERK
1975

I Sprechstudien:

Ostern — Himmelschlüssel — Sommerbäume — Sternschnuppen
— Sommerfaden — Verlassenes Moor — Gespenster — Einsames
Licht

II Copa Syrisca
III Sieben Gedichte von Bert Brecht:
Jahr für Jahr — Das Ölfeld — Die Apokalyptischen Reiter —
Moderne Legende — Karsamstagslegende — Epilog — Die
Liebenden

Ergänzende und weiterführende Ausgaben

Gunild Keetman

Rhythmische Übung
Erstes Spiel am Xylophon
Spielbuch für Xylophon im pentatonischen Raum:
I: für einen Spieler
II: für zwei Spieler
III: für großes Xylophon
Üb- und Spielstücke für Pauken
Spielstücke für Blockflöten Ia, Ib
Stücke für Flöte und Trommel I, II
Spielstücke für kleines Schlagwerk
Spielstücke für Blockflöten und kleines Schlagwerk

Gunild Keetman — Minna Ronnefeld

Erstes Spiel auf der Blockflöte
mit Anweisung für Zusammenspiel und Improvisation

Carl Orff

Einzug und Reigen
für Blockflöten, Zupf- und Schlaginstrumente
(aus der Musik zum Olympischen Festspiel 1936)

Klavierübung
Geigenübung I, II

Hermann Regner

Bläserübung
I: für Blechbläser
II: für Blechbläser und Schlagwerk

Lieder für die Schule

Eine Sammlung von Volks- und Kinderliedern in einfachen
Sätzen für Schulwerk-Instrumente (7 Hefte: Keetman, Orff,
Willert-Orff)

289

Gunild Keetman

        Elementaria
        Erster Umgang mit dem Orff-Schulwerk
        Klett Stuttgart 1976 (1970[1])

Wilhelm Keller

        Einführung in ,,Musik für Kinder''
        1963 (1954[1])

EDITIONS IN OTHER LANGUAGES

English edition

        Music for Children

        English Version adapted by Margaret Murray

Volume I   Pentatonic
Volume II   Major: Drone bass — Triads
Volume III   Major: Dominant and Subdominant Triads
Volume IV   Minor: Drone Bass — Triads
Volume V   Minor: Dominant and Subdominant Triads

Supplementary: Eight English Nursery Songs

        Eighteen Pieces for Descant Recorder and Orff-Instruments

        Nine Carols

        Wee Willie Winkie and seven other songs

        The Christmas Story

        Sayings — Riddles — Auguries — Charms (Gertrud Orff)
        Studies for Speech

        Carols and Anthems I, II (ed. by Isabel Carley)

        Elementaria: First acquaintance with Orff-Schulwerk Gunild
        Keetman (trans. Murray) Schott, London 1974

Welsh edition   *Argraffiad Cymraeg*

        Addasiad Cymraeg o Rhan I a II
        Ymarferiadau Llafar gan Ellinor Olwen Jones

Volume I   Pentatonig

Canadian edition   *Music for Children*

        English Adaptation by Doreen Hall — Arnold Walter

Volume I   Pentatonic
Volume II   Major: Bordun
Volume III   Major: Triads
Volume IV   Minor: Bordun
Volume V   Minor: Triads

        Teacher's Manual (Doreen Hall)

Supplementary: Nursery Rhymes and Songs (Orff-Hall)

        Singing Games and Songs (Hall)

        Songs for Schools (Keith Bissell)

American edition	*Music for Children*
	Orff-Schulwerk — American Edition
Volume 1	Pre-School
Volume 2	Primary
Volume 3	Intermediate
Supplementary:	Ten Folk Carols for Christmas (Jane Frazee)
	Eight Miniatures for Recorder and Orff Instruments (Hermann Regner)
	Four Psalm Settings (Sue Ellen Page)
	Kukuriku Hebrew Songs and Dances (Miriam Samuelson)
	Circus Rondo (Donald Slagel)
French edition	*Musique pour enfants*
	Version et adaptation françaises par Jos Wuytack — Aline Pendleton-Pelliot
Volume I	Pentatonique
Volume II	Majeur
Supplementary:	Chansons originales françaises extraites de l'oeuvre complète
	Chansons enfantines (Orff-Keetman) Quatorze chansons originales françaises
	Dix Chansons Françaises (Wuytack)
Italian edition	*Musica per bambini*
	Edizione italiana elaborata da Giovanni Piazza
Volume I	Manuale
Volume II	Esercizi
Volume III	Testi e canti
	Verlag: Suvini Zerboni, Milano
Spanish edition	*Música para Niños*
	Montserrat Sanuy — Luciano Gonzáles Sarmiento
	Versión original española basada en la obra de Carl Orff y Gunild Keetman
	Introducción al Orff-Schulwerk
Volume I	Pentatonico
	(Verlag: Unión Musical Española, Madrid)
Latin-American edition	*Música para Niños*
	Adaptatión Castellana para Latino-América realizada por Guillermo Graetzer
	Introducción a la práctica del Orff-Schulwerk
Volume I	1. Teil Pentafonia — Preparatorio 2. Teil Pentafonia — Intermedio
	(Verlag: Barry & Cia., Buenos Aires)
Supplementary:	Altindianische Tänze
	Indo-Amerikanische Tänze

291

Portuguese edition	*Musica para Crianças*
	Versão Portuguesa Maria de Lourdes Martins
Volume I	Pentatonico
Volume II	Bordões e acordes
Supplementary:	Canções para as escolas

Brazilian edition	
Supplementary:	Canções das crianças brasileiras (Hermann Regner)

Netherlands edition	*Muziek voor kinderen*
	Nederlandse bewerking Marcel Andries/Jos Wuytack
Volume I	Pentatonisch
Volume II	Grote Tertstoonsoort - Bourdon (Andries)
Volume III	Grote Tertstoonsoort-Dominanten (Wuytak)
Volume IV	Kleine Tertstoonsoort-Bourdon-Toontrappen (Wuytack)
Supplementary:	Nederlandse Volksliederen bewerkt door Marcel Andries
	Elf Nederlandse Volksliederen in oudi modi bewerkt door Jos Wuytack

Danish edition	*Musik for børn*
	Dansk Version Minna Ronnefeld
Volume I	Pentatonik
Supplementary:	Danske Børne - og folkesange

Swedish edition	*Musik för barn*
	Svensk Version Daniel Helldén
Volume I	Pentatonik
Volume II	Dur: borduner
Supplementary:	Ung Kirkoton I, II (Auswahl aus Musik für Kinder mit schwedischer Textunterlage)
	(Gehrmans Musik-Förlag Stockholm)

Czech edition	*Ceskà Orffova skola*
	Ilja Hurnik — Petr Eben
Volume I	Zaĉátky
Volume II	Pentatonika
Volume III	Dur — Moll
	(Verlag: Edition Supraphon Prag)

Greek edition	
Supplementary:	Griechische Kinderlieder und Tänze I, II, Polyxene Mathéy

Japanese edition	*Music for Children*
	Produced by Prof. Naohiro Fukui,
	Director of the Musashino Academy of Music, Tokyo
Volume I a	Rhymes and Singing Games
Volume I b	Rhythmic-melodic exercises
Volume I c	Instrumental pieces
Volume II a and b	Drone Bass
Volume II c	Triads
Volume III a and b	Dominant and Subdominant
Supplementary:	Japanese children's songs in settings by Gunild Keetman
	Japanese children's songs in settings by Shoji Kato
	(Publisher: Ongaku-No-Tomo Sha Inc. Tokyo)
African Edition	
(Ghana)	Orff-Schulwerk in the African Tradition
	African Songs and Rhythms for Children — a Selection from Ghana by W. K. Amoaku

Unless otherwise stated, all editions are published by Schott

EXAMPLES ON PHONOGRAPH RECORDS

The record series Musica Poetica (Harmonia Mundi) comprises ten 30cm records with accompanying texts and explanatory book in German, English and French.

I   Pentatonik I
II   Dur — Bordun/Stufen
III   Dur — Dominanten
IV   Dur — Unterdominanten; Pentatonik II
V   Äolisch — Bordun
VI   Dorisch — Bordun; Phrygisch — Bordun
VII   Moll — Stufen: I u. VII, I u. III u. a.; Moll — Dominanten
VIII   Moll — Unterdominanten; Lydisch; Mixolydisch
IX   Tanzstücke für Bläser und Schlagwerk
X   Sprech-Szenen, Laudi, Balladen

Extracts from the complete edition of Musica Poetica

Musikalisches Hausbuch	HM/BASF
Guten Morgen Spielmann	HM/BASF
Frühlingsbeginn — Sommergewinn	HM/BASF
Winterzeit, Märchenzeit	Marcato
Kinderlieder, Spiele, Reime	Marcato
Die Weihnachtsgeschichte (The Christmas Story)	HM
Het Kerstwonder (Die Weihnachtsgeschichte), niederländische Übersetzung von Vic Nees	DECCA
Kerstspel (Die Weihnachtsgeschichte) niederländische Übersetzung von Pierre v. Hauwe	CNR
Orff-Schulwerk Musik für Kinder I und II	Electrola (Dacapo)
Music for children I, II English Version by Margaret Murray	Columbia

Musica poetica, Edition française
(distribuée en France par CBS Disques

Rondes & Comptines	HMU
Printemps	HMU
Tournois & Troubadours	HMU

Hudba pro Mládez ,,Schulwerk''
Ilja Hurnik — Petr Eben   Supraphon

Japanische Kinderlieder
Keetman/Kato   Toshiba Records JK

ORFF-SCHULWERK SOCIETIES
AND THEIR PUBLICATIONS

Orff-Schulwerk-Gesellschaft in der BRD e. V.
Hermann-Hummel-Straße 25, D-8032 Lochham bei München
Bundesrepublik Deutschland
>   Orff-Schulwerk-Informationen

Gesellschaft der Förderer des Orff-Schulwerkes
Morzgerstraße 67, 4-5034, Salzburg, Österreich
>   Orff-Schulwerk-Informationen

American Orff-Schulwerk Association
Dept. of Music, Cleveland State University, Cleveland, OH 44115 U.S.A.
>   The Orff Echo

Orff-Schulwerk Society of Canada
University of Music, Edward H. Johnston Building, Toronto 5, Ont., Canada
>   Music for Children — Musique pour Enfants

Orff-Schulwerk Society of England
31 Roedean Crescent, London SW15 5JX, England
>   Bulletin

Orff-Schulwerk Association of Queensland
11 Mirbalia Street, Everton Hills, Queensland, Australia
>   Bulletin

Orff-Schulwerk Association of New South Wales
School's Music Centre, Blackfriars Street, Chippendale, 2008 Australia

Orff-Schulwerk Association of Southern Africa
58 Dawn Drive, Northcliff View, Johannesburg 58, South Africa
>   The Orff Beat

Stichting Orff-Werkgroep-Nederland
Koornmarkt 10, Delft, Niederlande
>   Wegwijzer in het Orff Schulwerk

BIBLIOGRAPHY

Some extracts or full translations of the following are available in English. Enquire through your local Orff-Schulwerk Society.

CURT SACHS: Geist und Werden der Musikinstrumente. Berlin 1929

— Vergleichende Musikwissenschaft. Leipzig 1930, Heidelberg 1959^2

— Eine Weltgeschichte des Tanzes. Berlin 1933

EBERHARD PREUSSNER: Allgemeine Musikerziehung. Heidelberg 1959

DOROTHEE GÜNTHER: Der Tanz als Bewegungsphänomen. Hamburg 1962

JAHRBÜCHER DES ORFF-INSTITUTS an der Akademie ‚Mozarteum', Salzburg, hsg. von Werner Thomas und Willibald Götze. Mainz; I: 1962 (auch in engl. Sprache); II: 1963; III: 1969

ORFF-SCHULWERK-INFORMATIONEN, hsg. vom Orff-Institut an der Hochschule ‚Mozarteum', Salzburg (Redaktion: Lilo Gersdorf). In unregelmäßiger Folge seit 1964

BARBARA KREYE: Musik und Bewegung. Bildbericht über die Arbeit mit dem Schulwerk (Texte K. H. Ruppel und S. Böhm). München 1965

BARBARA HASELBACH: Tanz und Bewegung. Stuttgart 1970

HANS WOLFGART (Hsg.): Das Orff-Schulwerk im Dienste der Erziehung und Therapie behinderter Kinder (Sammelband mit 19 Beiträgen). Berlin-Charlottenburg 1971

BARBARA HASELBACH: Tanzerziehung, Grundlagen und Modelle für Kindergarten*, Vorschule und Grundschule. Stuttgart 1971

10 JAHRE ORFF-INSTITUT. Eine Dokumentation. Hsg. vom Orff-Institut (Redaktion: Lilo Gersdorf). Salzburg 1972 (mit Literaturverzeichnis)

ORFF-SCHULWERK HEUTE. Bestandsaufnahme und Ausblick. Bericht über eine Informationstagung 1972. Hsg. vom Orff-Institut (Redaktion: Hermann Regner). Salzburg 1972

GERTRUD ORFF: Die Orff-Musiktherapie. München 1974**

HANS WOLFGART (Hsg.): Orff-Schulwerk und Therapie (Sammelband mit 18 Beiträgen). Berlin 1975

SYMPOSION „ORFF-SCHULWERK 1975". Eine Dokumentation. Hsg. vom Orff-Institut (Redaktion: Lilo Gersdorf). Salzburg 1975 ( ) Orff-Schulwerk-Informationen 16)

SUSE BÖHM: Spiele mit dem Orff-Schulwerk, photographiert von Peter Keetman. Stuttgart 1975

KLAUS W. OBERBORBECK: Die Literatur zum Orff-Schulwerk' bis 1975. IN: Orff-Schulwerk-Informationen 17. Salzburg 1976

WERNER THOMAS: Musica poetica. Gestalt und Funktion des Orff-Schulwerks. Tutzing 1976

*English edition *Dance Education* (trans. M. Murray) Schott/London 1978
**English edition *The Orff Music Therapy* (trans. M. Murray) Schott/London 1978

INDEX OF NAMES

PHOTOGRAPH SOURCES

Karl Alliger, München 91, 94, 95, 102, 104, 106, 107, 108, 137, 138, 139, 140, 141, 142, 143, 144, 219, 261, 278, 279

Frobenius-Institut, Frankfurt 16

Ines Hauth-Disclez, Munich 223, 224, 225

Peter Keetman, Breitbrunn am Chiemsee 151

Koninklijk Instituut voor de Tropen, Amsterdam 93

Barbara Kreye, Munich 222, 260, 262, 263, 264, 269, 270, 271, 272, 273, 274, 275

Städt. Musikinstrumentensammlung, Munich 95, 107

Heinz Tichawsky, Munich 234, 235, 236, 237, 238

Bust of Eberhard Preussner (p. 267) by Josef Magnus, Salzburg; Photo: Anni Madner

All photographs not acknowledged here come from the Orff Archives

This book could not have come into being without the help of Gunild Keetman, without the energetic, organising collaboration of my wife, Liselotte, and without the untiring sense of commitment of my archivist, Hannelore Gassner.

It is dedicated to the memory of Dorothee Günther, Eberhard Preussner, Curt Sachs, Oskar Lang, Karl Maendler, Klaus Becker, Will Götze and Walter Panofsky.